WHISKEY

WICKEDNESS

WHISKEY

WICKEDNESS

RIDEAU RIVER VALLEY

OF

- CARLETON, LANARK, LEEDS AND GRENVILLE COUNTIES -

- NO. 1-

BYTOWN (OTTAWA) 1815 to 1845

BELL'S CORNERS 1815 to 1845

RICHMOND, FRANKTOWN

MANOTICK,

NORTH GOWER, OXFORD MILLS

KARS, BURRITT'S RAPIDS,

KEMPTVILLE,

MERRICKVILLE

By
Larry D. Cotton

Larry D. Cotton Associates Limited
Lanark, Ontario, Canada

Email: ldcotton@sympatico.ca
or
Larry.Cotton@WhiskeyAndWickedness.com

Published in Canada by Larry D. Cotton Associates Limited

Cataloguing in Publication Data

Cotton, Larry D.

Whiskey and Wickedness - Rideau River Valley, Ontario

No. 1

Communities – Ottawa, Bell's Corners, Manotick, Kars, North Gower, Kemptville, Oxford Mills, North Augusta, Bishop's Mills, Burritt's Rapids, Merrickville.

ISBN 978-0-9784875-0-8

Layout and formatting of book done by Robert Eady & Scott Ivers of MousePoint, Lanark, Ontario.
Web: www.mousepoint.com / Phone: (613) 259-5797

Printed and bound in Canada by
Doculink International, Ottawa, Ontario

ACKNOWLEDGEMENTS

Ms. Erin Poulton, Education Officer and Ms. Donna Keays-Hockey Goulbourn Township Museum; Ms. Ann MacPhail and Bill Bowes, Library Resource Centre, Perth Campus, Algonquin College; Genealogy Room; Ottawa Room, Ottawa Public Library; Ms. Coral S. Lindsay, Ms. Susan Mckerral and Georgina M. Tupper, Rideau Township Archives, North Gower; Douglas Hendry, Director of Archives, and Sylvie Morel of the North Grenville Archives, Acton Corners; Gordon and Jean Newman, Oxford Mills; Mr. & Mrs. Patterson, Oxford Mills;., Scott Ivers and Robert Eady of MousePoint Computers, Lanark, Ontario; Tom Robinson and Martha Prince of Doculink International.

And to Monique Picotte, who worked hard to provide the digital photography for many pictures in the book, with patience and good humour.

OTHER PUBLICATIONS BY AUTHOR

Whiskey & Wickedness Vol. I - Barrie, Ontario
Whiskey & Wickedness Vol. II - Orillia, Ontario
Whiskey & Wickedness Vol. III - Muskoka & Parry Sound
Whiskey & Wickedness Vol. IV - Collingwood & Clearview Township, Ontario
Whiskey & Wickedness Vol. V – Grey County, Ontario

This is No. 1 in a series of six books titled "Whiskey & Wickedness". The sequels to this publication are:

No. 2 – Rideau River – Smiths Falls to Westport;
No. 3 – Madawaska and Bonnechere River Valleys;
No. 4 – Mississippi and Carp River Valleys'
No. 5 – Upper Ottawa Valley of Renfrew County;
No. 6 – Montebello to Fort William, Quebec

TABLE OF CONTENTS

LIST OF FIGURES

INTRODUCTION

A·Scotchman who had put up at an inn, was asked in the morning how he had slept. "Troth muum," replied Donald, "nae very well either; but I was muckle better off than the bugs, for no a ane o' them closed an e'e the hale nicht."

This is the story of the taverns in the Rideau River Valley from Ottawa (Bytown) to Merrickville. It explores the lives of the people impacted by them.

Taverns served two fundamentally different roles in the days of early settlement: they were an oasis of civilization in the heart of a primeval wilderness. They served as places of warmth, comfort, hospitality and companionship. But inns also had another dimension – one of brutality, profanity, rowdy behaviour, drunkenness and sometimes murder.

The Ottawa River and its tributaries served as the first transportation corridors into the interior of Eastern Ontario and Western Quebec. One of those tributaries -the Rideau River and its valley played a vital historical and economic role in the development of Canada as a nation and Ottawa as its capital city. The story of how this happened involved the founding and building of a new society in the Rideau River Valley and along the Rideau Canal - unlike any other in North America.

In 1823, the Bathurst District in Upper Canada (Ontario) took in an immense geographic area, stretching along the Ottawa River from present day Ottawa, northwest to Deux Rivieres. The District also encompassed most of the north shore of the Rideau River, including the present day areas of the western portion of the City of Ottawa and the County of Lanark.

Neighbouring Johnstown District stretched along the south shore of the Rideau from Kemptville to Westport.

Sparsely settled in the 1820's beyond a few scattered urban places such as Hull, Perth, Lanark, Richmond and Merrickville, several events would change this quietude. The end of the Napoleonic Wars in Europe; the construction of the Rideau Canal between 1826 and 1832 and the beginning of the economically lucrative square timber trade with Europe, triggered large scale migration and settlement into the Ottawa Valley.

Alcohol played an important role in the early social and economic development of the Districts of Bathurst and Johnstown. A significant by-product of the construction of the Rideau Canal and the economic and social impact of the square timber industry was the proliferation of taverns throughout the two districts and the resultant drunkenness and violence.

The humble country taverns and pretentious hotels of the rising towns and villages of the nineteenth century were the venues that promoted societal change in attitudes and customs related to alcohol consumption.

Along many quiet country roads and busy arterial routes, nothing remains to mark their ghostly presence, but memories and legend. The crossroads and stream crossings where they once gathered in abundance stand in silent solitude. Men and women, who sang and drank and fought and sheltered within their welcoming walls, fill the graveyards - patrons who died prematurely from the evil influence of drink.

Today a few relicts still stand along the main streets of the towns and villages of the Ottawa Valley. At one time public houses were the centre of social, political and economic life in the community; today they often appear drab, run down and out of place - archaic vestiges of another time and circumstance, waiting for a new lease on life or the wrecker's ball.

SETTLEMENT OF THE DISTRICT OF BATHURST: CARLETON AND LANARK COUNTIES

Colonial Government policy played a very significant role in the development of urban settlement in the locations of Ottawa, Richmond, Franktown, Lanark and Perth. The War of 1812 with the United States of

America, convinced British authorities that if they did not want to lose Canada to the Americans, they had to take strategic action. The necessity of developing new settlements composed of loyal settlers and infrastructure to foster military security and economic growth, were absolutely essential.

The end of the long Napoleonic War in Europe in 1815, presented a challenge and an opportunity to Great Britain – what to do with hundreds of thousands of military personnel that were no longer required in Europe? The cost to the British Treasury of the military pensions that these men would soon begin to collect was also another acute concern. An agricultural depression across the countryside of England, Wales, Scotland and Ireland, placed many people on parish relief with no hope or prospects for their children. Retired or disbanded military men saw no future in returning to the villages of their origins, while the industrial revolution in the large centers offered few opportunities for them.

Fortunately, the British Government and Crown, recognized the challenges and opportunities afforded by colonies such as Canada. The Government owned millions of acres of wilderness land, which it had secured through treaties with the aboriginal people. At the same time, no revenues of significance were being generated from these lands, which the burgeoning population of the ever-expanding United States, eyed enviously.

Offering disbanded military men land in Canada, in return for placing them on "half pay", seemed to be the answer. Providing supply depots and urban places to administer the new lands being settled was essential to facilitating, the settlement and public infrastructure works required to support, the large movement of people into the wilderness of the Ottawa, Rideau and Mississippi River Valleys.

Building roads, planning new towns, erecting saw and grist mills and constructing the greatest engineering feat in the world at the time – the Rideau Canal – were necessary for its success.

The history of the City of Ottawa and the Counties of Carleton, Renfrew and Lanark, in terms of European settlement, began with the formation of the District of Bathurst in 1823. It encompassed present day Lanark and Renfrew Counties plus most of the present day City of Ottawa. Initially,

Ottawa comprised Upper Bytown and Richmond Landing in Nepean Township and Lower Bytown in Gloucester Township.

The Bathurst District Capital, which housed the judicial and administrative buildings and functions, was the Town of Perth in Lanark County. Neither the City of Ottawa or its early predecessor, "Bytown", existed in 1822. The military supply centres of Richmond and Franktown, together with the District capital of Perth, were the only urban places of consequence.

Richmond Road: Its Beginnings

Since one the principal purposes of constructing Richmond Road was to provide an alternative linkage between Perth, the District Capital and Montreal and Quebec City, connecting it to the Ottawa River became a priority. A safer supply route and second line of defense against any American invasion, weighed heavily in the minds of the military authorities after the experience of the recently fought War of 1812-1814. With the military settlement of Richmond quickly being brought to fruition, constructing the next half of the Richmond Road westward from Richmond to Perth, became a priority.

The overland route cleared through the bush of Nepean Township and then into Goulbourn Township to the Jock River, where the Town of Richmond would be plotted out, became known as the "Richmond Road". Today it follows the same approximate route.

The construction of the Richmond Road westward from the Ottawa River began in September 1818, with the military settlers forming the principal labour component.

Colonel Cockburn, the military officer responsible, described the efforts in a report in November 1818:

> *"The road, or rather the track, which is opening between Richmond and Perth, runs in the direction of the base line of the new military townships, and generally speaking about two miles*

from it. It is on this road, and as nearly as circumstances will admit in the centre of the township of Beckwith, that a provision store is to be built ….. when this road is opened each of the new townships will be equally eligible for a settlement… "[1]

The Perth-Richmond Military Road proceeded westward out of Goulbourn Township into Beckwith Township in Lanark County. Another supply depot for incoming settlers was considered essential and thus the village of "Franktown" was planned for that purpose.

The taverns established along the length and breadth of the Richmond Road beginning at the Ottawa River and the Baseline Road beginning at the Rideau River and connecting with the Richmond Road, served as important linkages to facilitate the initial construction of the Canal at the Hog's Back.

Figure 1: Map of the Area Traversed by Richmond Rd.

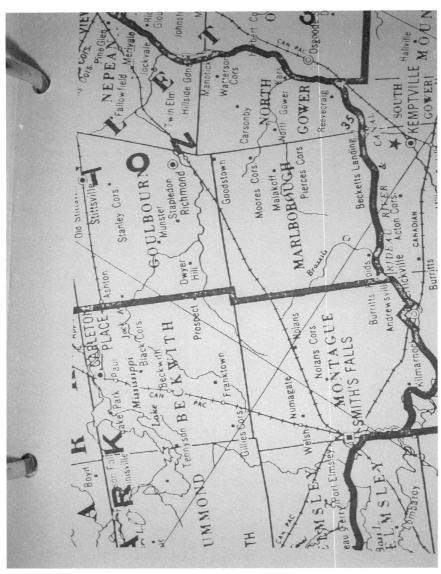

Charles Magee began keeping a public house on the Richmond Road near Britannia Mills about 1830. He prospered in this location, becoming quite wealthy compared to many of his inn keeping peers. Magee acted as host until the early 1840's when James Magee took over in 1845.

Incendiaries were a serious problem for all innkeepers. Drunken customers, who were refused further service by the landlord, often took their revenge by starting a fire in the stable when leaving the premises. When innkeeper Edmond Wood on the Richmond Road, lost his barn to arson in March 1838, he was informed that a fellow publican, Charles McGee was behind the fire. A war of words began.

ADVERTISEMENT.

Bytown, 9th June, 1838.

MR. CHARLES M'GEE:

SIR,—Having publicly stated my belief that you were concerned in the burning of my Barn, on the fourth of March last, I deem it my duty to you as well as to myself to declare, in an equally public manner, that my suspicion arose from the misrepresentation of individuals who I have since discovered are unworthy of belief, and to whose falsehoods, being at the time only slightly acquainted with you, I was but too ready to lend an ear.

I have now no hesitation in declaring, that I am well satisfied that the burning of my barn was an act in which you had no hand, and that I am not aware of any thing injurious to your character. I am willing to pay the costs of the action you have commenced against me, and trust that under the circumstances you will discontinue the same.

You are at liberty to make what use you please of this letter.

I am, Sir,

Your obedient Servant,

EDMOND L. WOOD.

The Founding of Ottawa

Ottawa is a sub-arctic lumber-village converted by Royal
mandate into a political cock-pit.
-Goldwin Smith

Noted historian Edwin Guillet described the Capital City of Canada thusly:

"Bytown, as Ottawa was first called, owed its early importance
to lumbering and as the terminus of the Rideau Canal, an
important military work intended to avoid danger from possible
depredations of the republican and democratic Americans. At
first Bytown was intended to be fortified, but instead it became a
wild and turbulent village, full of lumbermen, Irishmen and
liquor. Charles Daubeny, who was there in 1837, noted that the
Irish retained 'their lawless habits, and in this wild country it is
not very easy to bring them under the dominion of law'."

The original location for the formation of an urban settlement, where the City of Ottawa stands today was the Chaudiere Falls. A location on the Ottawa River, just below the formidable Chaudiere Falls was chosen as the landing area. It became known as the "Richmond Landing". A government road was proposed from this location to provide access to the interior, particularly the Town of Perth. Richmond Landing was the location where traffic on the Ottawa River disembarked and portaged around the Falls or utilized the Richmond Road to proceed inland to Perth. An early collection of taverns appeared at Richmond Landing, to service this transient population.

Isaac Firth and Andrew Barrie erected the "Union Hotel" at Richmond Landing on the Ottawa River in 1819. Firth initially worked on cutting out the Richmond Road from the Landing to the Richmond military settlement, before starting tavern keeping. A Perth newspaper described the setting in 1828 as follows:

"The Union Hotel ... commands a most interesting view of the mountains and scenery in the vicinity of Hull, the islands and banks of the noble Ottawa, the magnificent Falls of the Chaudiere ... " [2]

Firth's tavern became a popular gathering place for the gentlemen of Uppertown, when Bytown started to become established in 1826. After Isaac Firth's death, his widow, "Mother" Firth was a fixture for decades at this location in Upper Bytown.

Caleb Bellows constructed a store and a wharf at the "Landing" about 1820, while a small distillery established by Ralph Smith functioned nearby. Smith supplied whiskey to various taverns setting up along the recently opened Richmond Road.

An ever increasing amount of square timber traveled down the Ottawa River annually and had to by-pass the Chaudiere Falls. Timber rafts had to be disassembled above the Falls, with the heavier pieces such as oak transported by oxen overland down the "landing", where they were re-assembled into cribs and eventually rafts. Hundreds of often idle rivermen congregated at this point on the Ottawa River, for weeks at a time, waiting for the rafts to be reconstructed so that they continue their journey to the market at Quebec City. Drinking and carousing at the taverns in close proximity to the Falls, occupied their time, as they waited.

As the amount of commercial activity increased along the Ottawa River, additional public houses appeared at this locale –Charles Hollister opened a tavern in 1824, as did Jehiel Collins in 1828 at the Landing.

Together with the lands above the cataract, this riverfront parcel was acquired by Captain John LeBreton and L.P. Sherwood in 1820 at an auction. These men had ambitious commercial plans for their new property. Two tenants occupied small portions of these lands at the landing, when LeBreton and Sherwood purchased the parcel – innkeepers Isaac Firth and Andrew Berry, who opened their public house – "Union Hotel" in 1819.

LeBreton and Sherwood surveyed a part of their lands on the Flats into a community which they called the "Town of Sherwood" in 1822. Unfortunately, the Colonial authorities directed by Governor Lord

Dalhousie, attempted to thwart the efforts of the two entrepreneurs at every turn, claiming that these lands were intended for public purposes.

In fact, Governor Dalhousie acquired a large tract of high land adjacent to Sherwood's on the east and north of the property of Nicholas Sparks, the next year in 1823. Assisted by Lt. Colonel John By upon his arrival in 1826, plans for a town site, hospital and barracks for the British military were made on the Governor's instructions. These lands are now known as "Parliament Hill" and are occupied by the Parliament Buildings and offices of the Federal Government of Canada.

In 1826, the Governor also facilitated the opening of a timber channel around the Chaudiere Falls and the construction of bridges connecting the islands between Hull and the Chaudiere. Some of these works were on LeBreton and Sherwood's lands or had negative financial implications to both men. Neither landowner received financial compensation from the Colonial authorities for this high-handed treatment of their private property rights.

Entrepreneurs such as Ralph Smith operated a ferry boat service at LeBreton Flats and ran a distillery to supply the raftsmen on the Ottawa.

Surveying Town Site of Ottawa

The significant administrative role of the Bathurst District, Court of Quarter Sessions sitting in Perth, had in the founding of the City of Ottawa is interesting. In June 1830, the Justices determined the geographic area to be encompassed within the community of Bytown and appointed a surveyor to lay out the streets.

Upper Bytown, which comprised the area on the west side of the Rideau Canal, was high, dry and Scottish Protestant. Lower Bytown, on the east side of the Canal was primarily low lying, swampy land – and Irish and French Canadian Catholic. The men of commerce, military and civil administration resided in Upper Bytown.

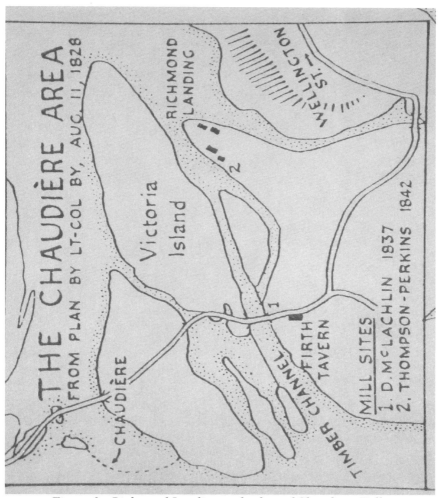

Figure 2: Richmond Landing at the foot of Chaudiere Falls

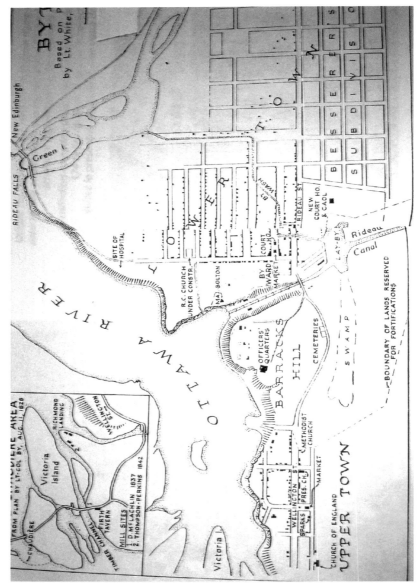

Figure 3: Upper and Lower Bytown as surveyed by Colonel By

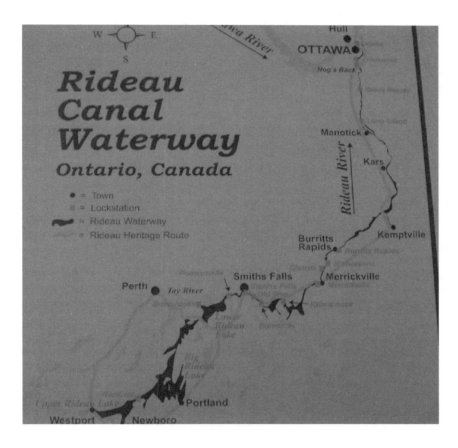

Figure 4: Rideau Canal Waterway – Communities between Ottawa and Westport

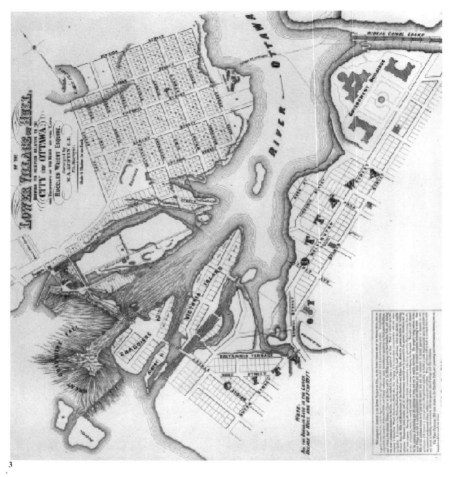

PLAN OF THE LOWER VILLAGE OF HULL AND OTTAWA ALONG RIVER
-1882-

CONSTRUCTING THE RIDEAU CANAL

The arrival of Colonel By and the engineering and survey corps at Richmond Landing in the summer of 1826, would have a profound impact on the future development of the Rideau River Valley and Ottawa in particular.

As men and material accumulated for the monumental construction project, a "boom" type of atmosphere pervaded the entire Richmond Road. Shelter and accommodation was in high demand, and numerous entrepreneurial types stepped forward, setting up taverns to service the canal workers.

Beginning in the summer of 1826, construction of the Rideau Canal would encompass the next six years until 1832. Thousands of labourers, stone masons, carpenters, teamsters, contractors and engineers worked along the two hundred kilometre route of the canal at numerous locations, installing locks, building lock houses, military fortifications, cutting trees, draining swamps and a myriad of other tasks.

The Impact of The Canal Construction

The commercial beginnings of the present City of Ottawa, date back to this time. The formation of the community of Bytown and later Ottawa, did not take place until the early beginnings of the Rideau Canal about 1826. A large influx of labourers from Ireland began to arrive that year, erecting rough shelters or moving into emigrant sheds in the vicinity of Richmond Landing and the area that would become known as Lower Bytown or Lowertown. These men would form the backbone of the workers constructing the Canal over the next six years. Scottish and Irish stone masons would also add their skills to this engineering masterpiece. Together this group, although highly transient in nature, formed the population base that established the community of Bytown.

A description of the appearance of Bytown in 1827 by a recently arrived immigrant provides a startling contrast to the City's appearance today:

"... the site on which that beautiful City now stands was then a complete wilderness – they had just then commenced to cut down the trees, and grub up the stumps to begin the Canal. ..."[4]

Colonel By surveyed the land around the start of the canal works, rented lots to settlers and workers flowing into the area, opened up streets and adopted regulations for the building of houses in Upper and Lower Bytown. This "town planning" activity created physical order for an urban community that started to take formation along the Ottawa River, adjacent to the location where the Rideau Canal construction was beginning to take place.

Less than two years after By's arrival, the following description of the "town" was given in the summer of 1828:

"The streets are laid out with much regularity, and of a liberal width ..... the number of houses now built is about 150, most of which are constructed of wood; ...... On the elevated banks of the Bay, the Hospital, an extensive stone building and three barracks stand conspicuous;..... In addition to homes and structures of stone, there were also a few shanties in what came to be known as Corktown, a settlement which up along the sides of the Deep Cut, made up of the Irish workmen who were responsible for much of the essential hand labour which actually built the Canal."[5]

When the Canal opened in 1832, Bytown's population was 1,500.

Figure 5: The Rideau Canal where it outlets at the Ottawa River. Source Edwin Guillet, "Taverns and Inns" Vol. 2

𝔇isease, 𝔙iolence and 𝔇eath

Many projects were under construction simultaneously along the two hundred kilometre corridor. Problems with the labour force were a continual issue from Bytown to Kingston. The large group of construction labourers comprising mostly poor, illiterate Irish were a particularly troublesome component of the entire work force. This group would later become collectively known as the "shiners", when they moved on into the square timber trade upon completion of the canal works.

Riotous conduct, intemperance and violence toward authority plagued the project from the very beginning. Incidents such as the following provide an example of the trouble created by a handful of malcontents amongst the workers.

"A gang entered the powder magazine of Mr. Crayton, canal contractor at the Hog's Back in December 1829. Stealing two kegs of blasting powder, they took it the home of a person then absent, with whom they had previously quarreled. Setting fire to the powder by means of a candle applied to a slow match, caused a premature explosion. The person setting the charge was blown up and afterwards found a blackened corpse about thirty feet distant. The building where the powder charge was detonated and two other adjacent structures were totally destroyed."[6]

Intemperance was aided and abetted by some of the Canal contractors. For instance, Thomas Dalton owner of the Kingston Brewery, provided beer for the workers as partial payment for labour, as part of his financial contribution to one of the contractors. Other distillers and brewers financially assisted contractors in the same way, to maximize their profits on contracts.[7]

In April 1831, Colonel By found it necessary to remove in a summary fashion from a government building which he loaned for use as a bakery, a man called Hill, who was found to be selling spirituous liquors to the men on the works. Hill was given twenty-four hours in which to get out of the building. When he had not moved in forty-eight hours, the British military commander ordered a platoon to remove the offending goods. The door had to be forced open and this was observed by one of the local Magistrates, though he did not interfere. The sergeant and corporal in command of the party, which carried out the raid were then arrested by the civil authorities. The next day, Colonel By himself was reputed to have been arrested by the Deputy Sheriff as being the instigator of a riot, 500 pounds sterling being requested for his bail until the next Assize. No record of the outcome of these charges can be found.[8]

Many men died during the construction. Diseases, construction accidents, violence and intemperance killed perhaps a thousand men employed on the project. Many references in early newspapers during that period provide only a tiny glimpse into the human side of the story. An example is the following short item in the Brockville Recorder newspaper in May 1830. "An inquest was held on the body of Thomas Murphy, carpenter at Edmund's Rapids, near Merrickville, Rideau Canal. The verdict of the Jury was that the deceased came to his death by intemperance."[9]

Numerous men were discharged for drunkenness. Often they gravitated to the hostelries of Bytown, along the Richmond Road and in the Town of Perth. These public houses also operated as recruitment centers for additional labourers. A man might be fired from the works at Bytown, only to be rehired by a different contractor at Merrickville, a few days later. Ex-military men such as a Sergeant Adamson, who had to be discharged for repeated drunkenness, was provided a letter from another military man dismissing him, signed by the salutation "your obedient servant". [10]

Sites along the Canal route which required the construction of locks, often developed into hamlets, partly because of the demands for accommodation, food and other necessities by dozens or perhaps hundreds of labourers in a locale for months or longer.

A description of an observer, who traveled along the construction line of the Rideau Canal in February 1830 of the site of the future community of Manotick, was the following: "At Long Island, there is the appearance of the commencement of a solid village not observable in other places. The contractor has built a good stone house in which he resides and a large stone store, which will be used as a residence for a lock keeper, when the canal is in operation." [11]

At Manotick, some of the work was completed in early 1830.

> "When the great dam at the foot of Long Island was completed
> in February 1830, the contractors gave a hearty round of drinks
> to the workmen present 'all of whom as our informant says,
> appeared peaceable, good humoured and contented. The
> bottom of the lock was finely frozen, and the smooth surface was
> considered an eligible arena for a ball, which was held in open
> air that evening'. A few days afterwards, Colonel By came to
> the spot and on being informed of the sociality and good conduct
> of the workmen, gave them a 'liberal treat'."

The Perth correspondent recording these events further commented:

> "Now it is really gratifying to record such a scene as this, when
> compared with the insubordination, riots, feuds and dissensions

which frequently occur at other stations on the line of works,
still more so to know, the rapid progress which is occurring in
this great undertaking toward completion. " [12]

REIGN OF TERROR: SHINER WAR IN BYTOWN 1830 TO 1843

The lawlessness in the Bathurst District is perhaps best exemplified by a group known as the "Shiners", who terrorized the frontier society of early Bytown and the Ottawa Valley for over a decade.

A combination of factors, brought a large group of destitute Irish emigrants in the mid 1820's into the Ottawa Valley. Large scale public works projects such as the construction of the Lachine Canal; Rideau Canal and military fortifications such as Fort Henry and other works protecting the Rideau Canal, provided plenty of employment between 1826 and 1832. But when these works were completed, several thousand men were suddenly jobless.

Bytown Magistrate, George Baker, chaired a public meeting in Upper Bytown in October 1833, which passed a resolution calling for the establishment of a new district centred on Bytown. A petition forwarded to Bathurst District Council in Perth appeared to have no effect. [13]

The Shiner's reign of terror thus began in earnest in 1835. Over the next two years alone, more than fifty people lost their lives in the ensuing violence. As a group the Shiners coalesced behind Peter Aylen's leadership.

"Not the least of the things Peter Aylen offered the Shiners was
sensual enjoyment. For a people all too familiar with poverty,
the lavish entertainment proferred by Aylen was highly alluring.
Food and drink were always available at the Shiner leader's
home as were pleasures of a more exotic nature. Women were
supplied the raftsmen, to satisfy the lusts pent-up from a winter
of enforced celibacy. On some occasions, it was reported, Aylen
imported prostitutes from Montreal for his men. The orgies ...
were extended, exuberant affairs, which often combined the dual
pleasures of debauchery and insult to the respectable
community. For instance, after sexual appetites were satisfied,
the Shiners were known to fill their women with liquor until they

collapsed insensible. Then the girls were stripped naked and arranged on the public sidewalk – well illuminated with candles so they might be seen be the shocked townspeople. "[14]

The organized mayhem in Bytown, spread throughout the Ottawa Valley, as the Shiners moved to secure control of employment on the rivers in the Districts of Bathurst and Ottawa.

"By late May of 1835, unrest in Bytown had reached unprecedented proportions. All winter the people of the town, the entrepot of the Ottawa timber trade, had been bracing themselves, awaiting the annual visitation, the annual affliction, of the raftsmen who came each spring from high up the Valley to roister and riot in the streets of Bytown. ... But never before had their coming brought such organized violence as it did in 1835. For the Irish timberers now had a leader, and a purpose. Peter Aylen ... timber king, ambitious schemer, had set himself at the head of the Irish masses, had moulded them into a powerful weapon. He had given them a purpose: to drive the French Canadians off the river and thus guarantee jobs and high wages in the timber camps to the Irish.

Confident in their numbers, Aylen and his followers swaggered the streets of Bytown, brawling and drinking on the sidewalks, savagely beating anyone who dared challenge them. The town suffered under this reign of terror ... the Irish mob, glorying in the name of the Shiners, seemed in complete control. ... "[15]

The problems in brawling Bytown were particularly disturbing to both the inhabitants of the community and the Magistrates trying to maintain law and order. The rule of law seemed desperately lost, except in a few isolated instances:

"..... five persons were committed to jail in this town charged with various offences, by the Magistrates of Bytown, in which place these desperados have been for some time past residing. We have heard of acts of grossest brutality imputed to some of the gang, ... We will merely mention the charges ... Committed

for having violently assaulted and ravished an old Indian squaw."

Charged with this offence were Jerry Ryan, John Hollahan and Michael Hoolahan. Magistrate George Baker managed to arrest these men. A brother of one of the prisoners, threatened to kill the chief witness against the accused and rescue their compatriots. Again, the bold Magistrate stepped in and arrested Edward Ryan and Joseph Benson for threatening to blow out the brains of William Brown, the Crown's chief witness. Fortunately, the military authorities permitted the prisoners to be held in the garrison jail in Bytown, until they could be transported to Perth.[16]

The "Shiners" brought from Bytown and lodged in the District Gaol in Perth commenced undermining part of the building and had nearly completed their plan of escape when Mr. Young, the gaoler, very opportunely caught them, and had them handcuffed. [17] One of the convicted felons, Jeremiah Ryan, was banished from the colony for life, as part of his sentencing. A couple of years later, he was back in Ottawa and in trouble with the law.

The Violence Continues

Until this point in time, the anarchy had principally been confined to Lower Bytown on the east side of the Rideau Canal.

"While French-Canadian labourers were being abused, the gentry of the community shook their heads in disgust and grumbled about the Irish misbehaviour. ... in 1835, the forces of order and disorder were in fine balance."

The detached attitude of Scottish, Protestant Upper Bytown, changed abruptly in the summer of 1835, when the violence spread from Catholic Lower Bytown, across the Rideau Canal onto the turf of the gentry.

Prominent Perth barrister and solicitor, Daniel McMartin, on a business trip to Bytown in 1836, was accosted by a group of Shiners on the street led by Peter Aylen. McMartin not being a solid, robust man, received a fierce beating from Peter Aylen, who repeatedly struck and kicked him.

Managing to escape, McMartin ran for his life along Wellington Street with his assailants closely on his heels.

Finally, reaching John Chitty's Hotel in respectable Upper Bytown, the innkeeper quickly took charge. Instructing McMartin to go up to his room, effectively saved McMartin's life. The Shiners threatened Chitty, who waved a pistol in their faces, as he told them to get out. Taken aback by the temerity of the publican, the Shiners left with a promise to burn the premises to the ground.

> *"The rule of the gentility in the town, and the aspirations of the Shiners, had come into direct conflict."*

Arresting Aylen proved to be a challenge. Although the authorities initially were able to apprehend him, Aylen was rescued by a large group of his followers. For the next two or three days, a mob of raftsmen, armed with guns and headed by the escaped prisoner, Peter Aylen, paraded the streets. Anonymous letters were circulated threatening violence to the public house of John Chitty. After some trouble, Aylen was captured again, this time by the military. Incarcerated in the guard house in the barracks, Aylen remained under heavy guard and very early the next morning sent off under a strong escort of armed Constables, along the Richmond Road to the Bathurst District jail in Perth.[18]

> *"However, in Bytown itself the furious raftsmen were in almost complete control. They paraded the streets, screaming threats at the magistrates, boasting they would burn down Chitty's Hotel, where the injured lawyer McMartin was in residence. Only the reading of the Riot Act and the calling out of the garrison prevented the destruction of the hotel."*

Unable to secure bail in Bytown or in Perth, Aylen remained in jail. His followers decided to switch their focus from revenge on McMartin and Chitty, to rescuing their leader.

> *"His supporters being under the idea that Aylen would be sent to Perth by the Rideau Canal, commenced an assault upon the crew of one of the steamboats, and the disabled the engineer and*

*several others. A subsequent attack was made upon the crew of
the Shannon steamboat ...and the Captain ... severely beaten."[19]*

Within a short time, Aylen was out of jail and the violence continued.
Bytown Magistrate, half pay officer and the Postmaster, George W. Baker,
wrote to the Government in June 1835 and tendered his resignation,
because of futility of not being able to control the anarchy in the streets.

Baker informed the Colonial authorities that the laws could not be
enforced, but he could not rely on twelve men in the whole village to aid
him in time of trouble. In fact, out of a dozen men deputized as
Constables, only four could be counted on in an emergency, according to
Baker. The Magistrate stated that protecting his own family during the
period of anarchy would require his full concentration. In his letter, the
despair showed through:

> *"I cannot Sir describe to you the situation of the town. If I
> could, you would deem it incredible and it is becoming daily
> worse ... No person whatever can move by day without insult, or
> at night without risk of life – thus whole families of unoffending
> people are obliged to abandon the Town, and nothing except
> Military Patrol will succeed in arresting the evil, and dissipating
> the general alarm ... I have not moved without Arms since the
> 14th May ... "[20]*

The state of affairs described by Baker, quickly showed themselves to be
accurate. In July 1835, Constable Dixon attempted to arrest a Shiner
wanted on a charge of rape. A large crowd of people gathered around the
confrontation.   Three Shiners brutally beat Dixon and rescued their
colleague. Fear prevented the witnesses from intervening.

Notwithstanding , the occasional legal setback, the Shiners under the
organizational direction of Peter Aylen, continued to strengthen their hold
over Bytown and the upper Ottawa Valley throughout 1835.

> *"The measure of control enjoyed by the Shiners, once Aylen had
> organized them, was demonstrated by their domination of the
> Union Bridge over the Ottawa River. The toll-keeper, one*

McClellan, established a 'shibbeen' selling liquor to the raftsmen. Attracted by his wares, the Shiners took over control of the span, insulting and assaulting travelers and demanding payment for passage over it. Although the government owned the bridge, no one dared intervene to stop the outrages. All too frequently bodies were found below the bridge, victims of the playful celebrations of the Shiners above. "[21]

The degree of crime and lawlessness within the Bathurst District during the year 1835, perhaps is best exemplified by the number of criminal cases and convictions, that the Grand Jury dealt with in a single Court of Quarter Session held at Perth in December 1835. The Jury rendered four verdicts of murder and eight verdicts of manslaughter during one Session.

Acts of random, senseless violence appeared in almost every edition of local newspapers during the 1830's. Here are examples:

On an August evening in 1836, a mob of Shiners attacked four men passing along a street in Lower Bytown, by hurling large stones at them. One the men received a severe cut in the face. Another industrious farmer, named Heron, had his skull fractured, and left in an unconscious state. [22]

In October 1837, a party of Canadians had assembled in a small shanty on the banks of the Rideau Canal, about two miles from the Sapper's bridge, to indulge in the innocent amusement of dancing. During the evening, a party of Shiners armed with paddles and sticks, burst open the door, and without provocation or the least warning, commenced beating and thrashing the occupants. The Canadians thinking the assailants too many for them, and panic struck, fled from the scene of riot with all the dispatch they could make. A man named Biggar, who had leased the shanty, became the chief object of attack. He was severely cut and bruised about the head, so as to endanger his life, the safety of which it was said he owed to the roof of the shanty being so low as to prevent the free use of the bludgeons of the villains. ...[23]

When the body of a man was discovered in the ice of the Rideau Canal in April 1838, a Coroner's Inquest took place. It was determined that the man was a blacksmith named Thromp, who disappeared in the fall of 1837 after a fight with a group of Shiners. A party of French Canadians were enjoying themselves at a dance in a shanty, when a group of Shiners arrived and began to assault the inhabitants. Thromp heard the commotion and tried to intervene on behalf of the Canadians. He subsequently was murdered by the Shiners for interfering with their "sport". The verdict of the inquest: "That the deceased came to his death by being forced or driven into the Rideau Canal, and there drowned; and that one Richard Fitzgerald, one Pat Malone, one James Hast, one Pat Carroll, lumber men, with others, (names unknown) were accessory to forcing or driving the deceased into the Canal."[24]

Even the local newspapers appeared to be intimidated by the Shiners. The Bytown Gazette on February 23, 1837 provided these comments respecting the violence:

> "... that the reports of disturbances in Bytown have been very much exaggerated at a distance; ... we must admit, that many lawless characters have been going about, and many acts of wanton aggression have been committed. ... but from the want of a jail where delinquents could be confined; ... and the vicinity of Bytown to Lower Canada, allows frequent instances of escape from justice, which leads to complaints against the Magistrates..."

Innkeepers Dispute With the Shiners

An innkeeper named Joseph Galipaut ran a popular tavern in Lower Town frequented by French-Canadian raftsmen. As part of the intimidation of their enemies, the Shiners staged a raid on Galipaut's public house in the spring of 1833. Peter Aylen's bodyguard, a giant named Martin Hennessy, led the raiders in the attack, mounted on his horse which he rode into the bar room. As the patrons scrambled for safety, Hennessy armed to the teeth, began shouting threats and obscenities. His Shiner crew flooded into the inn.

In a quick, decisive moment, innkeeper Galipaut pulled a pistol from under the bar and shot at the mounted intruder. Hennessy was hit in the face. Tumbling backwards off his horse, he fell hard onto the bar room floor, blood streaming from the region of his eyes. Blinded and infuriated,

Hennessy was quickly picked up by the Irish attackers and carried out of the premises. Galipaut became a marked man and time was on the side of the Shiners.

A second attack on Galipaut's public house occurred in the spring of 1835. Again, the courageous owner retrieved a pistol, and shot and wounded one of the invaders, a man named Matthew Power. Aylen decided to change tactics. He contacted the only Irish Catholic Magistrate in Bytown, Daniel O'Connor and convinced him to arrest Galipaut on the charge of attempted murder. O'Connor being sympathetic to his countrymen and perhaps ..... intimidated, had the innkeeper arrested. This posed a serious problem though. Where could Galipaut be detained? He wouldn't make it to the District Gaol in Perth, alive. There was no jail in Bytown except the military facility, where the Parliament Buildings now stand. But the arrest appeared to be purely a local criminal matter which fell under the jurisdication of the civil authorities. O'Connor pleaded a case of incipient insurrection to the military authorities, which they reluctantly accepted. Galipaut safely ensconced in a garrison cell, worried about the safety of his family and business.

Released from jail in June 1835, Galipaut, abandoned his public house and fled for his life from Bytown. A week later, a group of Shiners burned his premises to the ground.[25]

Innkeeper, John Little, who conducted the "Victoria Hotel" on Sussex Street in Lower Town, also aroused the ire of the Shiners in 1835. Little was assaulted by Shiner, Thomas Macaulay, in his public house. Assault charges were laid against the Shiner, who was pursued by Magistrates Daniel Fisher, George Baker and D.R. MacNab. Macaulay fled to Peter Aylen's house, where Aylen tried to prevent their entry. Getting past the homeowner, they found another Magistrate, Daniel O'Connor inside. O'Connor informed his colleagues that without a warrant, they had no authority to enter. In the ensuing argument, Aylen threatened the three invading Magistrates. O'Connor's position as a Magistrate was certainly undermined by being discovered socializing in the home of a criminal.

The Shiners decided to blow up his Little's Hotel partly as an act of revenge, but perhaps to also make an example out of him. A Shiner named "hairy Barney", who was a well known ruffian in Bytown, volunteered to carry out the retribution. Hauling a keg of gun powder to the back of the public house, Barney lit a match. An instantaneous explosion occurred, blowing the unfortunate Barney into several distinct portions. A newspaper account of the event stated: "..... His remains lay there all blackened and seared as they were, for some time, and not one of his confederates would acknowledge him, until at little shoemaker came along, who recognized the shoes he had on, which he had made for him. ..."[26]

The Shiners were not through with tavern owner John Little though. Next an attempt to set fire to the premises was made. A suspect, Michael McNaughton, was arrested on suspicion of an attempt to set fire to the hotel. Committed to stand trial for arson, McNaughton was escorted under strong guard to Perth to be held in the District Gaol, while awaiting his trial.[27]

The Shiners and Orangemen War

The Orangemen and the Shiners were mortal enemies. Whenever, individuals or groups belonging to either party were found in close proximity to one another, a fight would result. Sometimes, neither group recognized any bounds of civilization, when it came to attempting to harm the other party.

Prior to the annual parade held on July 12th by the Orange Order, to celebrate the victory in Ireland of the Protestant army under King William of the House of Orange, over a Catholic army in 1688, Magistrate R.S. Jamieson issued a proclamation in Bytown in July 1835 against rioting. When the Orange Parade was held in Bytown, a year earlier, several men were killed and numerous badly hurt in the ensuing rioting between the Shiners and the Orangemen.[28]

The Shiners attacked the wife and daughters of an Orangeman named Hobbs. They town and were returning to their farm on a sleigh when they were attacked by a drunken mob who beat them senseless with sticks. Mrs Hobbs who was pregnant tried to jump from the sleigh but her clothing snagged and she was dragged along the frozen ground while the Shiners continued to beat her.

The pregnant wife and daughters of an Orangeman named Hobbs had been shopping in Bytown in February 1837. While returning to their farm along the Richmond Road, they encountered a group of drunken Shiners who blocked their passage. Stopping the sleigh, the Shiners savagely beat all the members of the family with sticks, boots and fists. The frightened horses started to run away, dragging Mrs. Hobbs along the frozen ground. The Shiners ran alongside the rig, continuing to beat the pregnant woman as she was dragged behind the sleigh. Stealing the horses and sleigh, the outlaws finally left their battered victims, lying in their blood along the roadside.

Fortunately, none of them were murdered. The Shiners then attacked the horses. The next day Hobbs came into Bytown and recovered his team of horses, which had been mutilated. Their ears and tails cut off and one with a dreadful hole in its flank.[29]

The next day when Hobbs came into town he found the animals missing their ears and tails. He determined that the guilty Shiners were being hidden and protected by their friends in Corktown.

Revenge was in the air. This action galvanized the whole countryside against these outlaws. The neighbouring farmers were almost all Orangemen who were former soldiers in the British army. Within a week, the Orangeman Hobbs, enlisted a large group of heavily armed Orangemen from the surrounding countryside, to march on Bytown to capture a Shiner named Gleeson, who instigated the assault on the Hobbs' family. The Magistrates quickly convened a conference of war with the Orange contingent. Informing the Magistrates that the purpose of their visit was to assist the authorities to secure the arrest of Gleeson and his cohorts, they were told that the matter would be quickly looked into. The Orangemen retired to several nearby taverns to await further information and instructions.

Meanwhile, Magistrate Daniel O'Connor and the leader of the Shiners, Peter Aylen, decided that the best defence is a good offence. They spread a rumour throughout Lower Town that the Orangemen intended to attack the Roman Catholic population. This ruse worked. A large portion of the law-abiding Catholic population began to arm themselves for a fight, tricked into inadvertently supporting the Shiner outlaws.

Other Magistrates anticipating the potential bloodbath, quickly intervened and assured the Orangemen, that Gleeson would be immediately found and arrested. Using their legal authority, they formed a joint front against Magistrate O'Connor and Peter Aylen, and demanded Gleeson's immediate capture and arrest. Reluctantly, O'Connor carried out these instructions. Gleeson was conveyed to the District Jail in Perth to await trial. Gleeson was convicted of assaulting Mrs. Hobbs and fined ten pounds sterling.[30]

Hobbs wasn't finished with Gleeson and bided his time before administering his own version of justice. A year later he cornered Gleeson in a blacksmith shop where Hobbs proceeded to cut off Gleeson's ears. For the rest of his life Gleeson was the object of ridicule and was nicknamed 'Croppie'.

Problems between the Orangemen and the Shiners in Bytown continued throughout the 1840's. Every year the Orangemen celebrated the "Glorious 12th" of July with a colourful procession through the streets of many small communities in Ontario, followed by a picnic or dinner of the brethren at nearby taverns.

In July 1846, false rumors were spread through Bytown that an Orange procession would march on the streets of the Town on July 12th. In consequence, great numbers of Catholics came into Bytown, ostensibly for the purpose of intercepting them. A state of intense excitement soon gripped the community.

Anarchy continued to seethe just below the surface. Numerous threats of arson and physical harm were made to businesses and individuals, who tried to stop the lawless behaviour of the Shiners or obtain justice when Orangemen took the law into their own hands. Acts of personal and property damage between Protestant and Catholic activists continued on unabated throughout the 1830's and 1840's. Desecration of churches appears to be a new low in the fighting between the two groups. It is interesting to note that the reward advertised in a Bytown newspaper in 1839, indicates that the Magistrates in the Orange Protestant stronghold of Richmond and some of them Orangemen themselves, posted a reward of this nature.

REWARD.

ONE HUNDRED AND TEN POUNDS,

HAVING been placed in the hands of the Magistrates to be paid to any person or persons who shall give such information as will lead to the apprehension and conviction of the party or parties who were guilty of the disgraceful and sacriligious offence of breaking the Sashes and Glass of the Windows in the Roman Catholic Church, on Lot Number Twenty Three, in the Fifth Concession of Nepean. on the evening of Monday or Morning of Tuesday the 5th ult,

GEORGE LYON, J. P.
J. MAXWELL, J. P.
ANTHONY PHILIP, J. P.

Richmond, 15th April, 1839.   45.t

A prisoner was rescued from the police by a large mob. In the affray, a Magistrate McArthur and Constable Currie, were severely roughed up. On the same evening, a stranger from the country was severely beaten on the Sapper's Bridge by persons unknown. Six men attacked a young man walking to the Methodist Church and badly bruised him. A number of other men were attacked with provocation and houses attacked and windows broken in Bytown and New Edinburgh. Fire arms were discharged throughout the night creating terror among the citizens. A religious congregation was also shamefully disturbed.

A number of Magistrates together with Judge Armstrong and the Sheriff, tried by persuasive means to make peace, but instead were attacked and roughly handled. The military were then called upon and quickly arrived to support the civilian authorities. Several rioters were apprehended immediately and Special Constables sworn in to capture more of the trouble makers.

"... The disturbance and its consequence were occasioned by sectarian prejudice and party spirit, as some of those beaten

were marked out for ill treatment by party coloured
handkerchiefs which they wore. One of the Shiners who
attacked the hotel of John Elliott near the Hill, died from a
wound by a gun fired from the premise."[31]

Attempted Murder of James Johnston

Another Orangemen that ran afoul of the Shiner's was James Johnston, who emigrated from Ireland and settled in Bytown in 1827. Initially working as a merchant and auctioneer, Johnston interested himself in politics. A moderate Orangeman, Johnston ran for the Parliament of Upper Canada in the riding of Carleton on the Reform ticket in 1834 and 1836. Losing both those elections to the Conservative candidate, who also happened to be a fellow Orangeman, did not dampen his enthusiasm for public office.

Johnston petitioned the Lieutenant Governor to replace the biased Magistrates in the Bytown area – Scottish Magistrates with prejudicial views toward the Irish and Irish Catholic Magistrate Daniel O'Connor, whose bias favoured the Irish Catholics. This petitioning created a lot of enemies. Threats were made toward him. In October 1835, his house was set on fire and burned to the ground. Intimidation did not work.

James Johnston began publishing a newspaper in Bytown, the "Bytown Independent & Farmer's Advocate", which lasted only a short time period, but promoted his political candidacy. However, Johnston published the paper long enough to incur the wrath of of Peter Aylen because of its criticism of the Shiner's violent antics. A successful merchant as well, Johnston was harassed by the Shiners constantly. Eventually he laid charges against a group of men, who beat him up in his shop. Warned that he better drop the charges or be burned out, the threats became a reality in September 1835, when his store was torched by an incendiary.[32]

At the annual meeting of the inhabitants of the Township of Nepean in January 1837, the Shiners and Johnston met again. Convened at J. R. Stanley's tavern on Kent Street, Peter Aylen attended with a gang of his men. The Shiner "King" was determined to have only Shiners elected as Township officials. Addressing the meeting, Aylen demanded that everyone in the room be permitted to vote. The Chairman, James Johnston, informed Aylen that the law allowed only men owning unmortgaged property, the privilege of voting. An angry Aylen began shouting, which precipitated the start of a riot. In the ensuing melee, James Johnston again received a beating from the mob at Aylen's command. Complaining to the Lieutenant Governor, Sir Francis Bond Head, about Aylen and his gang in 1837, resulted in no action by the Governor but renewed attacks by the Shiners.

On the evening of the Orangemen/Shiner stand-off, in which the Shiner Gleeson was arrested for assault of the Hobbs' family, the Orangeman Hobbs stayed at his friend James Johnston's house. An angry and frustrated Peter Aylen, chagrined by Gleeson's arrest, heard about the arrangement for overnight accommodation and decided to extract revenge. Aylen hated Johnston and Hobbs about equally. Rallying his gang, they made their way over to Johnston's residence. Unable to force their way into the house, they decided to burn it down. Since the structure was made of stone, they were not able to accomplish that task either. The disconcerted mob hovered around the dwelling arguing about what to do attempt next. They decided to fire their pistols at the windows in frustration, which they did. Finally growing tired, they marched back to their hangout in Lower Town, to quench their thirst.

But Johnston's problems with the Shiners were not over. A month later, three Shiners tried to murder Johnston, who escaped by pulling out a pair of pistols. The next night, he did not get off as easily. Trapped on the Sappers Bridge that crossed the Rideau Canal, by the present day Chateau Laurier, Johnston jumped off the bridge and landed in soft snow up to his armpits. Completely helpless! Meanwhile, two of his adversaries, Patrick O'Brien and James McDonnell, fired pistols at his trapped body in the snow bank below the bridge. The third member of the gang, Thomas Burke, climbed down the bank to complete the mission, with the weighted butt of his whip. Burke did manage to fracture Johnston's skull in two places, before being driven off by a group of citizens, who came to the rescue.

The ensuing backlash in the community resulted in the arrest of the three Shiners, whom Aylen haughtily predicted would never stand trial. Transported to Perth with an armed guard of thirty soldiers, the men did not remain prisoners for long. An audacious group of Shiners stormed the Perth jail in May 1837. Faced with an armed and drunken mob, with murderous intent if he resisted the release of his prisoners, James Young, the Bathurst District Gaoler, freed the Shiners. The three escapees fled to the United States. Recaptured in New York State, they were tried for attempted murder and convicted to a terms of hard labour at Kingston Penitentiary.

James Young was subsequently charged with negligence in his official duties for allowing the three prisoners to escape. Appearing before a Grand Jury in Perth in the fall of 1837, Young was acquitted of all charges. The public and the officials of the District had lost faith in his ability to carry out his duties and never re-instated him. [33]

These incidents did demonstrate to the law-biding citizens, the need to establish a police force in Bytown – and appears to have been a strong catalyst toward that happening.

In the bitter Provincial election of 1841, Johnston once again ran as a candidate. This time he was opposed by his old arch-enemy, Daniel O'Connor, whom he beat. Elected again in 1844, Johnston steadfastly promoted the interests of Bytown and the need for a separate District for the Ottawa area.

Johnston resigned his Parliamentary seat, perhaps on a whim, after a drinking bout with his close friend, Parliamentary colleague and fellow Orangeman, Dr. William "Tiger"Dunlop. Trying to regain his seat in the ensuing by-election in 1846, Johnston lost. This experience appears to have strengthened his dependency on alcohol and led to his early death in 1849.

Finally a Response to the Anarchy

Maintaining law and order in Bytown with four part-time Magistrates, and no police force to back them, seemed to be an impossible task in 1835. As well, criminals could easily cross the Ottawa River into Lower Canada and into another jurisdiction with equally inadequate law enforcement, to escape Upper Canadian justice.

"Even if criminals were successfully arrested, the magistrates' problems were not at an end. The only jail was in Perth, forty miles away by canal or overland through the forest. The jail was remarkably porous, with a long history of successful escapes."[34]

In November 1835, a shantyman named John Stewart was arrested for assault and battery and incarcerated in the District jail in Perth. With the assistance of a friend outside, Thomas Murphy, the prisoner escaped. Shortly afterward Murphy was arrested for his role in the jail break, but a few days later he also escaped. Neither man was ever subsequently recaptured.[35]

Public safety became such a concern to the respectable citizenry of Bytown by the fall of 1835, that a vigilante committee was formed in Upper Town. The "Bytown Association for the Preservation of Peace" recruited over two hundred members into its organization. Its first step was to begin nightly patrols in Upper Town. Members armed themselves with whatever happened to be available. Official recognition or assistance to the Association was shunned by Lieutenant-Governor Colborne, who would not provide weapons or the use of the military prison to detain lawbreakers. Although this did limit the Associations effectiveness to some extent, the real problems related to public disorder were primarily focused in Lower Town, which the vigilantes avoided. Public safety in Upper Town did improve to a greater extent than the previous three or four years.

The vigilante committee managed to secure the Lieutenant Governor's tacit approval for the formation of an armed corps – the Bytown Rifles – which George Baker was appointed to lead. This special force was to be trained and armed to properly police the Village. However, mismanagement by Baker led to its early demise. A further issue that undermined the determination to secure public safety was the lack of a jail in the community to house law breakers. The military lock up could not be utilized for holding civilian law breakers.

The second step taken by a group of influential citizens would have a profound effect on the development of Bytown, as an urban centre surpassing the District Town of Perth. A public meeting convened in

Bytown in November 1835, discussed the issue of the great difficulty in the preservation of public peace. Constables and witnesses were required to attend Court in Perth but were not paid for their time or expenses. The disturbed state of affairs in Bytown, bordering on complete lawlessness, motivated the large group of influential citizens present to pass a motion supporting the separation of Bytown and its immediate neighbours from the Bathurst District. A committee was formed to collect signatures on a petition calling for the formation of a new District centred on Bytown.[36]

Six months later a group of Bytown merchants and prominent lumbermen, led by George Buchanan, formed a central committee in August 1836, empowered to frame a petition to present to the Legislative Assembly to establish a new District with Bytown as its capital. One of the reasons stated:

> *"That the expenses of conveying prisoners to Perth are so great,*
> *that many felonies and assaults are overlooked, from the*
> *inability of the people to raise the means necessary to bring*
> *delinquents to justice."* [37]

These moves for the formation of a separate district were accompanied with a debate regarding the location of a new jail to serve the new district. Initially, Richmond was chosen, to the consternation of a many people in Bytown, who considered it too far to convey prisoners. The major area of crime centered in Lower Bytown, therefore a more central location was thought to be necessary.

The conviction of several other Shiners in the fall of 1837 to terms in prison on charges of assault and rape, indicated that the anarchy so prevalent during the previous couple of years was coming to an end. The assault conviction of John Gleeson, who had injured Mrs. Hobbs, further reinforced the public's confidence that law and order was being slowly restored.

Shiner "King", Peter Aylen, recognized that his mob rule appeared to be coming to an end in Bytown toward the end of 1837. Selling his properties in Bytown and Nepean, Aylen moved across the Ottawa River to Aylmer in Lower Canada. Law enforcement in Quebec was a little more relaxed, just what the "King" desired.

INTEMPERANCE IN EARLY BYTOWN

Description of Early Bytown Taverns and Innkeepers

The early hotels of Bytown, clearly distinguished their location as being in Upper or Lower Bytown. They were considered separate and quite distinctly different urban entities for many decades in Bytown's early days.

Most of the merchants were lowland Scottish, while many of the numerous tavern keepers were former military men of Scottish, English and Irish background, on half pay or their widows. The French Canadians in Bytown at this early time were principally employed in the square timber trade and were attracted by the labour opportunities offered by the Canal construction, while almost all of the early lumbermen were Americans.

Ottawa author William P. Lett described in verse and immortalized a number of the prominent publicans of early Bytown in his "Recollections of Bytown and Its Old Inhabitants" published in 1874:

> *"And Julius Burpee gone! Well well*
> *He kept the old Rideau Hotel,*
> *Where man and beast could get the best*
> *And truly find the traveller's rest.*
> *Julius still might living be,*
> *Were it not for the 'barley bree'.*
>
> *John Little standing at his door –*
> *In Sussex Street where erst kept he*
> *An Inn of quite a good degree*
> *Of excellence in the old time.*
>
> *And Galipeau, who kept good whiskey,*
> *And old Jamaica to make frisky*
> *The visitors to his retreat*
> *On the east side of Sussex Street.*
>
> *And William Henry Baldwin, too*

Who first appeared in public view
At the old Albion, where, in state,
Bob Graham rules the roost of late.

John Chitty is a favourite name,
His old hotel was known to fame,
And travelers, from far and near,
Called at his temple of good cheer."[38]

John Chitty served on the committee that secured signatures and support for the formation of a separate District called "Dalhousie", that eventually separated Bytown and Carleton County from the Perth dominated Bathurst District.

Several Magistrates in Bytown sent the Provincial Secretary a letter in 1837, outlining the problems faced by them maintaining law and order in the community:

"Bytown being the focus of the lumber trade, is frequented at all seasons by great numbers of raftsmen, among whom are some desperate characters and others easily misled. The inhabitants are dependent upon the lumber trade and upon these men, and cannot, therefore, be prevailed with to act with energy against them. Those constables who perform their duty are always marked out for punishment ...

Generally speaking, the persons who commit these outrages are unknown, but if known and warrants issued for their arrest, they fly to the Lower Province (where we cannot touch them) but return again when they please, confident in their strength, and if they are arrested they are immediately rescued or manage to make their escape, from the defect in our constabulary force, and the great distance of the gaol (at Perth)."

Some tavern keepers, disgusted by the violence and lack of public safety or security, sold their buildings but refused to allow them to be used as taverns. Drinking was perceived by some conscientious publicans, to be a major cause of the large degree of social disorder in the community. Innkeeper, John Chitty appears to have been one of them.

TO LET, for the term of three or more years, and possession given on the first day of October next.

That extensive WOODEN HOUSE and Pre-. mises, situated on *Wellington Street*, Bytown, presently occupied as a *Hotel*, by John Chitty.

—ALSO,—

The STONE BUILDING adjoining the same, fronting on *Kent Street*.

The above premises is well adapted for the accommodation of a private family, or for a man in business. Is completely finished in the first style ; and from the extent of the accommodation, will be found well deserving the attention of any person wishing for such a situation.

The above Houses may be leased either separately or together — but not to be occupied as a *Hotel*.

For particulars, apply on the premises, to

JOHN CHITTY.

Bytown, June 20, 1836.   3-tf

With a population of 30,000 people in 1836, the Bathurst District encompassing the Counties of Carleton, Renfrew and Lanark, had 285 applications for tavern licences – and granted 178. Shop licences, which allowed sales of bottles from stores, were twice that number.

Bytown's population in 1836 comprised a little over 1,000 people. It had 15 licensed taverns out of the 178 across the District in 1836. Illegal outlets of whiskey distribution constituted a much larger number.

New Edinburgh

The Village of New Edinburgh was another distinctly separate urban area, lying east of Lower Bytown. Thomas McKay, a Scottish stonemason, worked as a contractor on the construction of the Rideau Canal. Acquiring land at the mouth of the Rideau River, MacKay constructed a saw mill, grist mill, a woolen mill and a distillery.

The large stone residence that McKay built for himself is now called "Rideau Hall", home of the Governor General. The sale of whiskey produced at McKay's distillery helped to pay for his new residence. McKay's grist mill at Rideau Falls in New Edinburgh was described as the "largest and best grist mill in America ..." in 1833.[39]

Around this industrial complex, he had his landholdings surveyed into a village, which he called "New Edinburgh".

A Mr. McTaggart also established an extensive brewery and distillery complex on the Rideau River at New Edinburgh in the 1830's. [40]

Upper Bytown, Lower Bytown, All Around Town

Publican's from the east side and west side of the Rideau Canal advertised their establishments. Some gained fame and fortune for the quality of their hostelries, while others gained notoriety. Here are some sample advertisements from the 1830's and 1840's:

ALBION HOTEL.

Lower Bytown

THE SUBSCRIBER begs leave to inform his friends and the Public, that he has leased the Large Commodious Stone Building, forming the corner opposite the District Court House and Gaol, Lower Bytown, which he has opened as a HOTEL, and respectfully intimates to those who may favor him with their patronage, that no exertions will be spared to give satisfaction. He can accommodate a few regular boarders with comfortable Bed Rooms and private parlours.— Travellers will find comfortable accommodation with good stabling for their horses. He also h spacious Ball Room—45 feet by 18.

ALLAN CAMERON

Bytown, Decr. 23d 1844.   2'

Dalhousie Hotel,

WELLINGTON STREET,

UPPER BYTOWN.

THE SUBSCRIBER begs leave respectfully to inform the Gentry and Travelling Community generally, that he has recently opened the above Splendid Establishment. This large and commodious HOTEL, being situated in the principal Street of Upper Bytown, in the immediate vicinity of the Crown Office, Banks, and Post Office, and within a few minute's walk of the beautiful and romantic Scenery of the Chaudiere Falls, is admirably adapted from its central position, for the accommodation of the Mercantile Community as for that of those who may be Travelling for pleasure alone. The Subscriber deems it almost superfluous to state, that his best endeavours and utmost exertions shall at all times be used to render this Establishment worthy of the Patronage of a discerning public, and that no expense shall be spared to make it as Comfortable in every respect as any other House of a similar description in the Province. CARRIAGES will be in constant attendance, to convey Passengers and their Baggage to and from the Steamboats.

JOHN L. CAMPBELL.

Bytown, August 24th, 1842. 7-tf

In order to be a successful hotel keeper in Bytown during the 1830's and 1840's, the host had to possess certain qualities. In the case of publican Robinson Lyon, who kept the "Exchange Hotel" in the mid 1840's, he was a wizard with a violin.

William Lett described the history of the premises and its occupants thusly:

"In fancy I away have stepped ...
In that old house remembered well,
After, as Joseph Kirk's Hotel,
Ere it was haunted by a sound
Which shed such melody around,
Sweet almost as the songs of Zion.
From violin of Robinson Lyon,
Who drew such music from its strings –
Scotch reels, strathspeys, and highland flings,
And Irish jigs in variation,
As made one feel that 'all creation'
Could scarcely match his wizard spell –
'Twas he played the fiddle well!"

Old army veteran, James Doran, ran the "British Hotel" in Upper Bytown. His approach to being a host to the public shines through in this ditty:

"And surly old James Doran, too,
A warrior of Waterloo,
Kept with a despot's iron hand,
The best hotel in all the land;
Who entered there of human kind
Was forced to leave his dog behind,
For Doran had a frowning face
For each and all the canine race."

Canine Sagacity

On a Saturday night in the spring of 1846, a man was attempting to make his way home from a rather lengthy drinking bout at a local tavern. The journey proved long and dry. Often he illustrated the theory most clearly, that all unsupported bodies have a tendency towards the earth's centre. He reeled into the barnyard of a farm stead near the road, in which a large and very furious watchdog was on a chain. How he managed to subdue the fierceness of the dog at such an hour cannot be understood, as no stranger dare approach within the range of its chain, even in daylight. But subdue it he did, for on the household going into the barnyard on Sunday morning, the dog was lying outside, and the man inside, the dog-house.

The more curious, fact is that the man was a complete stranger to the dog, and it can be accounted for only on the ground that the dog was passing wise, and pitied human frailty. Perhaps of all the astonished group who collected round his wooden tenement, no one was more amazed at his remarkable position and miraculous escape, than the "drouthy tenant" himself; who, on being hauled feet foremost out of the den he had usurped, and admonished of the fact that it was Sabbath morning, made the best of his way homewards, looking very foolish.

THE

BYTOWN COFFEE-HOUSE

This Establishment, situated on SUSSEX STREET

H MMEDIATELY on ascending from the Steam Boat Landing, in LOWER BYTOWN, is open for the reception of the Public and Travellers.

The Subscriber has spared no expence or exertions in making this Hotel one of the most respectable in the Canadas. The House is furnished in the best style—the appartments are so arranged as to afford accommodation to private families or parties—being in a situation immediately approachable, on the landing of Passengers from the Steam Boats. By unleviating attention to the wants of such as may favour him with their attention, the Subscriber hopes to merit a share of the Public patronage.

Every exertion will be made to have the Tables furnished in the best manner the Markets can supply, and the best of LIQUORS will be selected from the Montreal and Quebec markets.

LUCIUS BARNEY.

Bytown, 1st August, 1836. 119

The Irish community of Corkstown situated along the west banks at the "Deep Cut" of the Rideau Canal is remembered in verse:

CORKSTOWN

"In days of yore, with a call
Of where stands now the City Hall,
A village built of mud and wood,
In all its glory Corkstown stood,
Two rows of cabins in the swamp-
Begirt by ponds and vapors damp ...
There delved full many a hard case in
That Channel to the Canal Basin.
There then dwelt many a sturdy blade, ...
Lovers of poteen strong and clear,
In preference to rum or beer,
Sons of the sod who'd knock you down
For half a word 'gainst Cork's own town,
And kick you then for falling too,
To prove that the old mountain dew
Had frolic in it, raw and strong."

And the infamous Mother McGinty, who kept tavern in Corktown, was remembered by Lett's colourful prose:

"And there in a whitewashed shanty grand,
With kegs and bottles in each hand,
Her face decked with a winning smile,
Her head with cap of ancient style,
Crowned arbiter of frolic's fate,
Mother McGinty sat in state,
And measured out the mountain dew
To those whom strong attraction drew
Within the circle of her power
To while away a leisure hour."

Mother McGinty's management style should be studied by the students of the various Schools of Business in universities across the country, it appears to have been straightforward, decisive and effective for an illiterate, elderly Irish woman.

"She was the hostess and the host,
She kept the reckoning, ruled the roast,
And swung an arm of potent might
That few would dare to brave in fight;
Yet was she a good-natured soul,
As ever filled the flowing bowl;
In sooth she dealt in goodly cheer,
Half-pints of whiskey, quarts of beer, ...
The song, the dance, and the glass went round
The precincts of that classic ground;
And when bent on a tearing spree,
Filled full of grog and jollity, ...
While o'er them the athletic charms
Of the stern hostess's bare arms
Struck terror and kept order in
The revel's hottest, wildest din!
For cash or credit bartered she,
The prime ingredients of a spree;
And he stood always above par
Who never stone threw at the bar;
And when a man had spent his all,
She chalked the balance on the wall.
Figures or letters she knew not,
But what a customer had got
By hieroglyphics well she knew,
For there exposed to public view
Each debtor's tally great and small
Appeared upon the bar-room wall. ...
And woe to him, who soon or late
His tally did not liquidate;
For when her goodly company
Were all assembled for a spree,
She read off each delinquent's score,
And at his meanness loudly swore,
And threatened when he next appeared,
Unless the entry all was cleared,

To lay on future drinks a stricture, ...[41]

Figure 6: *"Russell House", Ottawa*

Figure 7: "Albion Hotel", Ottawa c.1875. Source: Edwin Guillet, "Taverns and Inns" Vol. 2.

Problem of Intemperance Finally Recognized

The combined population of Upper and Lower Bytown reached 1,300 in 1837. Getting a drink wouldn't be a problem - almost two hundred legally licensed taverns, over one hundred licensed "shops", dozens of distilleries and breweries, combined with an equal number of illegal outlets, could accommodate the thirstiest inhabitants in the Bathurst District. Actually, the limited public pressure to reduce the number of establishments that appeared to strictly-speaking – "groggeries" – seemed to have the ear of some District Councillors. Tavern licenses had been reduced across the region by 74 in 1837. Although it was quite a controversial decision, the politicians and some civic leaders wanted to determine the impact that it might have on reducing the violence, crime and accidental death that appeared to be associated with drinking.

Distillery owner, Captain Lewis, the Member of the Legislative Assembly for Upper Canada, representing Bytown, was appointed as a "commissioner" under the statute forming the Dalhousie District in 1839. His responsibility was to assist in the selection of a site for the jail and Court House for the new District being separated from the Bathurst District. The commissioners selected lands within the limits of Nicholas Spark's property, lying to the eastward of the Rideau Canal and a few rods in rear of Rideau Street, Lower Bytown.[42]

Ironically, some of Captain Lewis's "best" customers necessitated the construction of these facilities in the first place.

Bytown Fall Fairs

The first Bytown Cattle Fair held in 1830, offered the hope that the Town would provide a cash market for grain, cattle and other agricultural commodities. The problem of lawlessness ended that plan.

> *"... when the horserace which followed ... terminated in a riot*
> *with much head-breaking by the lawless Irish lumberjacks*
> *(Shiners). The authorities then forbade the holding of any more*
> *fairs at Bytown."[43]*

A newspaper man attending the Bytown Fall Fair of September 1840 commented:

> *"...we regret, as public journalists, to be compelled to express our disapprobation of the practice displayed ... of horse racing in the streets ... it betrays a gross degree of negligence on the part of our Magistrates, to tolerate a proceeding under their own eyes ... which they know is a public nuisance to disturb those engaged in their lawful pursuits, and dangerous to the lives of Her Majesty's lieges."* [44]

Bytown Total Abstinence Society

Alcohol shaped society through its impact on the laws, institutions and customs of the times. Cheap, plentiful and fashionable, whiskey consumption was widespread amongst all classes of people. It was difficult to avoid because almost all activities involved the casual and often heavy use of the stimulant. Weddings, funerals, work "bees" for raising barns, houses, cutting wood, clearing the forest, crop harvesting, sporting events, ploughing matches, fall fairs, elections and sporting events, provided reasons enough for public drunkenness.

In December 1836, the Grand Jury for the District of Bathurst in Sessions convened in the Council room in Perth. The Jurors were in a somber and anxious mood. The number of criminal charges related to assaults, rioting, arson, rape and murder could not be ignored. The growing lumber centre of Bytown seemed to be in a perpetual state of near anarchy and lawlessness, which stretched back three or four years. The District Gaol was filled with prisoners, but security was so weak that inmates routinely escaped custody. The District Magistrates were often threatened and sometimes assaulted, when they acted to curb the lawlessness. Their residences suffered from physical attacks, including arson. Constables attempting to enforce the law routinely were attacked and abused.

The Court deliberated on the causes of the current state of affairs and arrived at the following conclusion:

> *"The Grand Jury ... for the District of Bathurst in Sessions, this 21st day of December, 1836, feeling deeply the great and*

*growing evil in this District, occasioned by the number of
licensed and unlicensed houses, wherein ardent or intoxicating
drinks are sold, the keepers of which violate the laws of the land
by keeping tippling houses and keeping them open on the
Sabbath and at unseasonable hours, thereby encouraging the
growth of vice and immorality in a degree at present alarming
and revolting to all reflecting minds. We therefore, as Grand
Jurors, do call the attention of our public authorities to the
subject in general and recommend that the number of houses so
far as practicable be reduced that the laws now in existence be
in all cases of violation strictly enforced."[45]*

Formed in Bytown in 1838, this organization had a "total abstinence
pledge", unlike many of its counterparts. It produced a periodical titled
"Temperance Advocate" and a publication called the "Anti-Bacchus",
which was distributed to every clergyman and Magistrate in Bytown. In
its Annual Report for 1841, the following statements were made:

*"..... We mention the humiliating fact that we have yet in
Bytown, 39 places licensed to sell intoxicating drinks and
painful to state, a majority of our Magistrates are among the
vendors. Besides these, there are at least as many more
unlicensed kennels of infamy, which be plainly identified by the
pipes in the windows. ..... the practice of free circulation of
intoxicating liquors at our civic elections, a practice which
involves in itself a species of bribery at once dishonouring to the
giver and the receiver, and which is attended with circumstances
both demoralizing and dangerous to the peace of the community.*

*The scenes of riot, immorality and destruction which are
occasioned by drinking customs still in use, at our Fairs and
Agricultural Shows (to say nothing of the races, on which those
scenes are a more appropriate attendant), exhibit the
importance of the most decided and strenuous efforts to stay the
course of intemperance.*

*At the time of the last Annual Cattle Show, one individual lost
his reason and another his life, by accidents occasioned wholly*

by intoxication ....woeful wailings of widowed wives and
fatherless children."[46]

The newspapers commonly reported deaths related to intemperance. The body of a man named Charles Boyle was discovered dead in a school house in Marlborough Township in January 1841. It was supposed that he had been drinking too freely, sought shelter in the school and froze to death. He left a wife and young family to mourn his unfortunate end.[47]

In one respect, whiskey played a significant role in the movement toward establishing a separate District with Ottawa as its capital, allowing it to chart its own destiny, separate and distinct from Lanark and Renfrew Counties.

Critical Comments on the Choice of Ottawa as Capital City

An Ottawa Valley scribe quoted the comments of the influential and extremely powerful British newspaper, The Times of London, about the choice of the City of Ottawa rather than Montreal, as the new capital of Canada in 1862:

> "*Ottawa is the residence of a rough and disorderly set of*
> *lumberers ... that Her Majesty's advisors have been misled ...*
> *Ottawa is the head-quarters of the lumbermen because it is the*
> *wildest spot in Canada; that they are French-Canadians, and*
> *constitute three-fourths of the population of the 'village', which*
> *only contains 12,000 inhabitants. The lumbermen don't live in*
> *Ottawa – only 25% of the whole population is of French origin.*
> *The Irish in Ottawa exceed any other nationality in numbers,*
> *and it is just possible that they may be the 'rough and disorderly*
> *set' ...*
>
> *The Government buildings which are admitted to be 'grand,*
> *regal and ancient looking', will one day do 'for a lunatic*
> *asylum.'*"[48]

THE TAVERNS OF BELL'S CORNERS

Three "houses of public entertainment" appeared side-by-side on the north side of Richmond Road, where it splits with the Arnprior Road.

Beginning in 1815 and still in business in 1841, William Bell was a highly successful publican. He arrived before the advent of either the Richmond Road or Arnprior Road, established a tavern about 1815 in a "scooped" roofed log shanty east of the junction of the Richmond and Baseline Roads at Bell's Corners in Goulbourn Township. Bell worked on the construction of the Rideau Canal and lost his arm in a serious accident. Known as "one armed Will" because of the stump of an arm protruding from one sleeve on his shirt, Bell was a true host from the old school. He was generous and obliging in his dealings with the public and very protective of his family. Especially his beautiful daughter, Sarah, who eloped with the Irish hired man, Edward Rielly. Sarah and her husband, Edward Rielly, established a successful hotel in nearby Richmond, which still stands today.

Streams of wagons and sleighs and men bound for the shanties of the Upper Ottawa passed through Bell's Corners and filled up its hotels on an annual basis between the 1830's and 1880's. The Arnprior Road or "Whiskey Road", as it was known to travelers, began at Bell's Corners and went northwest into the lumbering regions of the Madawaska and Bonnechere Rivers. The Richmond Road running through Bell's Corners, would also be filled with farmers bringing their produce to the market in Bytown and later Ottawa and returning home.

Hugh Bell, erected a more substantial tavern at Bell's Corners on the north side of Richmond Road in 1834, to accommodated the growing traffic by his door. He played an active role in local political events serving as a Councillor, Assessor and Tax Collector. He often hosted Nepean Township Council meetings during the 1830's and 1840's. Bell conducted his tavern for a thirty year period ending in 1863. This is the present day site of Bell's Corners Public School.

West of Bell's hostelry, Robert Malcolmson established a tavern at the strategic intersection of Richmond and Base Line Roads in 1832, which he conducted into the 1850's. James Brown, a nearby tavern keeper, took over Malcolmson's premises during the 1850's and named it the "British Hotel". William Corbett acquired the property in the early 1860's and operated the public house until selling it to David Hartin in 1870. Burned in the conflagration of 1870, Hartin constructed a large new stone building on this site. Today it is the locale of "Al's Steak House".

John Steel, a Scot, settled in Nepean Township at what later became Bell's Corners in 1818. Establishing a stopping place about halfway between the Ottawa River and Richmond Village, it became a welcome resting place for travelers. His wife, Catharine Steel held the licence in 1823. Steel drowned in 1824. Steel's public house was taken over by William Boyd.

Gerard B. Chapman kept a licenced tavern, east of Richmond on the Richmond Road, where it meets the Jock River 1818.

John Robertson arrived at Bell's Corners in 1836 and opened a general store and tavern close to Bell's, to capture some of the traffic along this busy route. A few years later, a third Scot, Robert Moodie, another early resident of Bell's Corners, hosted a public house during the 1850's and 1860's on the north side of the Arnprior Road.

A man named Patrick Brophy came to his death in July 1861 under very suspicious circumstances. He had been drinking freely in the house of a tavern keeper named Bergen, near the Jock River in Nepean. He got into a quarrel with three young men named Thomas Quinlan, Patrick Quinlan and James O'Brien. Brophy was severely beaten by these men and lay for some time helpless. The patrons of the tavern alleged that they supposed him stupefied more from the effect of the liquor he had taken, than from the bruises received in the fight. On attempting to rouse him some time afterward, they found that he was dead. It was stated that he died from the effects of liquor and he was interred. Rumours of the quarrel having got abroad, a neighbouring magistrate caused an inquiry – a post mortem examination was held, and the surgical evidence warranted the step, warrants were issued against the Quinlans and O'Brien. The parties were found at their usual work, and quietly surrendered themselves to the authorities. On examination they were committed to trial. [49]

A tremendous fire in 1870 destroyed almost every building in Bell's Corners. The 1879 map depicts three hotels in a row on the north side of Richmond/Robertson Road intersection, with a toll gate to the east and another toll gate at the junction of Richmond Road and present day Moodie Drive.

Figure 8: William Bell's hotel at Bell's Corners, Ontario c. 1840. Today this is the site of Bell's Corner's Public School.

Figure 9: Hartin's Hotel, Bell's Corners, Ontario c. 1875. In 2007 it served as "Al's Steak House".

THE VILLAGE OF RICHMOND

The settlement of Richmond came about for several reasons. The military land grants being given to the east of Perth in Goulbourn Township, needed to be supplied from the Perth supply depot, which would create difficulties in provisioning for new settlers at such a distance. An alternative route into the interior needed to be established, for easier access. The Ottawa River provided a more direct and closer access point than the St. Lawrence River and the Brockville Road northward to Perth.

The Colonial authorities were also keen on the idea of opening a Rideau River corridor linkage between the Ottawa River and Kingston, for military and commercial purposes.

Arrival of the Chelsea Pensioners

A site on the Jock River, a tributary of the Rideau River (like the Tay River), was selected as the site for another planned town to function as a supply depot and commissariat for a large group of demobilized soldiers in 1818. The 99th Regiment of Foot left Lachine in August for their new land grants around Richmond.

The Jock River had significant water flow through its streambed in 1818. Sawn lumber was floated up to the military settlement under construction at Richmond, mostly from a saw mill at Merrickville. The lumber traveled down the Rideau River with all its rapids to the mouth of the Jock, and then floated up the Jock to the Richmond Road.

Military pensioners brought a unique set of challenges to the District because of their background. Many had been granted land based on an agreement to go on "half pay" for their pensions. The British Government reasoned that land was cheap and plentiful in Canada, while the expensive implications on the British Treasury of a large number of military men on full pensions could be avoided by this strategy. Other reasons were also at work. Having a large group of well trained but idle men at home, without work or prospects could lead to civil unrest.

At the same time, the recent War of 1812 with the United States, showed the rather ambivalent allegiance of the majority of settlers in Upper Canada to the Crown. Placing thousands of loyal and experienced military veterans as settlers in Upper and Lower Canada, would strengthen the British hold on these colonies, in the event of any future conflict with the Republic to the south.

Most were middle-aged and therefore not young or vigorous enough to tackle the difficult physical challenges posed by a solid wilderness of trees, wild animals and lack of any kind of society. Secondly, they were accustomed to giving and/or taking orders, which wasn't a skill set needed in the wilderness. Thirdly, making a living from the land or in a business was a foreign concept to most of them. In their former occupation they received a monthly salary and a daily ration of four pints of beer a day in the army or the equivalency in rum if they were in the navy. These daily alcohol rations predisposed the majority of them toward a dependency on alcohol. Of course the social times accustomed with the comradeship of their peers and drinking together, formed an integral part of their lives after years of service.

The Chelsea Pensioners were former soldiers, who had been injured or grown old in the services of the Crown, while the Greenwich Pensioners was instituted for seamen, who had left the navy. Both Chelsea and Greenwich Pensioners received pensions four times a year, including their alcohol rations. Commissariats were established in Bytown (still standing as the Bytown Museum beside the Rideau Canal across from the Chateau Laurier), Richmond, Franktown, Perth and Smith Falls, which distributed the pensions and alcohol rations, usually from a tavern in the community, often owned and operated by an ex-military man. These were occasions of much joviality and drunkenness, as the men congregated to collect their money and use up their alcohol rations.

Many ex-military men became tavern keepers. Unfortunately for them and their former comrades, they became their own best customers. Alcoholism, was a serious problem with this group of settlers, made worse by the hardships, loneliness and unfamiliarity of life in the forest. The closest tavern often became a home away from home for these men.

Early Taverns in Richmond

Sergeant-Major Andrew Hill opened an inn named the "Masonic Arms" in the fall of 1818, when the ex-military settlers began to arrive for settlement. A year later in August 1819, when the Duke of Richmond stayed at his humble public house, the landlord changed the name to "The Duke of Richmond Arms". Years later, when Maria Hill conducted the house it was known as the "Richmond Inn". Maria Hill conducted the "Richmond Inn" – 1837, 1839.

> *"The village of Richmond was a rather flourishing town for more than half a dozen years, …before Ottawa, began to take shape …Richmond had become a business and commercial centre of some consequence. There were at least a dozen good general stores, four breweries and two distilleries, a sawmill, gristmill, carding-mill, wagon-maker, blacksmith, harness-maker and cooper."*[50]

The Murray family perceived opportunity in the tavern business as well. Thomas Murray conducted an inn at Richmond in 1836. His brother James Murray did the same with his establishment on the Franktown/Perth Road 5 kilometres west of Richmond Village on the north east half of lot 15, and the south west half of lot 16, Goulbourn Twp.

FOR SALE.

THE following Lots of LAND, consisting of
TWO HUNDRED Acres, being the N. E.
half of 15, and S. W. half of 16, on the 3d Concession of *Goulbourn*, being situate within three
miles of RICHMOND, on the road to PERTH, on
which there is about 40 Acres of improvement,
and is now in a good state of cultivation, and well
watered by a beautiful Creek.

There is on the S. W. half of 16, a good dwelling HOUSE, BARN, OUT HOUSES, LIME
KILN, &c.

—ALSO,—

A Living Spring of WATER.

On the N. E. half of 15, there is a comfortable
DWELLING HOUSE.

The 200 Acres will be sold together, or singly,
(with or without the Crop now in the ground,) to
suit purchasers. Apply to

THOMAS MURRAY,
Inn-keeper, Richmond,

Or to

JAMES MURRAY,
Inn-keeper, on the Premises.
Richmond, June 27, 1936.   5 3w

During the period from 1835 to 1850, the simple taverns of Richmond's
early days such as the "Masonic Arms" of Maria Hill, began to be replaced
by public houses that had the audacity to call themselves "hotels". James
McLean ran a prominent "house of public entertainment" during this time
along with other proprietors such as Thomas Murray; James B. Lefevre,
Robinson Lyon and Denis Gaudette.

Distilleries and Breweries

Many pioneer communities could claim a distillery and perhaps a brewery,
as part of the local economic base during the 1830's. Often the local grist
mill operator conducted his milling services using the barter system. This
provided plenty of good grain that could be converted into other uses –
such as whiskey.

In the case of Richmond, however, it had an inordinate number of distilleries for its population size and location. Certainly the presence of the military Commissariat every three months, doling out pensions to the large group of ex-military settlers in the vicinity, had an impact on the per capita consumption of spirits.

HOUSE FOR SALE OR TO LET.

IN R¦chmond, on Lot No. 10. with a good large dwellingHouse, situated with good Stables, Sheds, yards and Barn, and a well and root house. Lot containing 11 acres of good cleared land, and four corner road leading to Bytown. Huntly, Perth and Kemptville, by
                                J. B. LEFEVER.
Richmond, Jan. 30, 1842.   1 6tf

During the 1830's and 1840's, Richmond could boast of at least three operational distilleries at any time, plus a couple of breweries. Charles Thompson, Thomas F. Daniel and George Lyon operated distilleries in the 1830's.

Captain George Lyon began a grist mill operation on the Jock River in Richmond in the early 1820's. Soon he expanded into distilling spirituous liquids, which were much in demand by the large number of retired military men in the vicinity.

Lyon held a "still licence" from the 1820's and into the 1850's in Richmond on Fortune Street, which allowed him to utilize a wooden 100 gallon barrel to make his brew in.

Lyon also became quite active in politics. Elected for the Conservative Party in 1832 and 1834, he fought to retain the waning power of the Village of Richmond, against the burgeoning commercial centre of Bytown. As a Magistrate in the Bathurst District, Lyon tried to maintain the rule of law in the Richmond area in the 1820's through to the 1840's. His brother, Robert Lyon was killed in the tragic duel in Perth in 1833.

He was also involved in the separation of Bytown and Carleton County from the Bathurst District and the formation of the new "Dalhousie District". Lyon died at age 61 in Richmond in 1851. The 1852 Census stated that the distillery belonging to the estate of the late George Lyon worked by water only during the winter months. It mashed 25 bushels of grain per day and produced an average of 65 gallons of spirits per day. Thomas Lyon took over its operation for the remainder of the 1850's.

Competitors of Lyons, such as Charles Thompson, left Richmond for Bytown by the latter part of the 1830's, where better opportunities were available in a growing central place. Small distillery operators such as Thomas F. Daniel in 1839, who produced spirits in a wooden 65 gallon apparatus, remained.

George Lyon's son, Robinson Lyon, watched his father's business affairs closely. By 1841, he began keeping a tavern in his hometown. It was the beginning of an occupation which he would successfully pursue for the next quarter century.

FOR SALE,

The Undermentioned Property, situated in the Village of RICHMOND, Bathurst District.

PART of a Town-ot, on which is erected a DISTILLERY, with Steam Boiler, Copper Worm, and all other necessary apparatus complete, and a building near it well fitted up as a Merchant's Shop, with storage for Grain, &c.

The above Property is situated in the centre of a fine Grain Country, and is well worthy the attention of a person possessing a small capital and desirous of turning it to advantage.

For further particulars, application to be made in Bytown to

CHARLES P. THOMPSON.

Bytown, 23th July, 1836.   t19

Notice.

MR. ROBINSON LYON having leased that commodious House in Upper Bytown, formerly occupied by Mr. Kirk, begs to inform his Friends and the Public, that he intends opening a HOTEL therein, by the first of May, when he will spare no exertion to merit a share of the Public Patronage.

He also purposes to keep a few HORSES at LIVERY.

Bytown, April 16, 1844.   41–tf

To Let.

TO BE LET, for a term of years, that well known Tavern Stand in Richmond, formerly occupied by Mr. Lefevre. Apply to Mr. ROBINSON LYON, RICHMOND.

Richmond, April 16, 1844.   41–tf

Figure 10: "Exchange Hotel" of Robinson Lyon in Ottawa, c.1844 which he took over after leaving Richmond. Source: Edwin Guillet "Taverns and Inns, Vol. 2".

An Orange Stronghold

Richmond was a stronghold of Orange power in the Bathurst District for many decades. The complete antithesis of the power wielded by the Shiners in Bytown, the Irish Protestant farmers of West Carleton enjoyed a drink and a fight, almost as much as their counterparts in "town". Conflict between these competing factions highlighted the social and economic tensions prevalent in early Ontario society.

Battles between the Orangemen of Richmond and the Shiners of Bytown became a commonplace event during the turbulent 1830's. In Richmond, Michael Burns was attacked by a party of "ruffians" and very inhumanely and cruelly beaten. On the following morning the unfortunate man died from the effects of the wounds he received.[51]

Old Thyme Elections: The "Open Ballot"

Elections of representatives to the Legislative Assembly of Upper Canada and later Canada West for the riding of Carleton and Lanark were violent and drunken affairs.

There was no such thing as a "secret ballot" until the 1860's. Electors cast their votes by an "open ballot" system. This required each man to stand before the returning officer in the polling station and verbally declare who he supported, before dozens and sometimes hundreds of witnesses. Everyone knew how each man voted.

Other critical factors played a significant part in the election process. Up until the 1860's, only one polling or voting station would be open for an entire electoral riding. And this polling station would most often be located in the bar room of a tavern. The polling station would be open for one week, so that people traveling from across the riding would have time to cover the distance from their homes.

Each candidate would keep "open house" for the week of voting at one or two taverns in the vicinity of the polling station. Potential voters would obtain free booze and food from each candidate attempting to influence how he would vote. Each candidate tried to keep the other man's supporters too drunk to reach the poll and his own just drunk enough to be happy.

Intimidation in the form of threats and physical violence were often openly used, particularly in front of the polling station. Employing bribery in the form of work contracts, location tickets, deeds for land often was also utilized.

Carleton was entitled to be represented by two members for the area now including the City of Ottawa west of the Rideau River from the 1831 election until 1842.

The 1831 election provides a typical example of the types of candidates and the issues. Captain George Lyon from Richmond combined with Captain John Bower Lewis to oppose Hamnett Pinhey of March and Dr. Alexander Christie of Bytown.

The growth of Bytown in population and commerce during the Rideau Canal construction period, created a decline in the fortunes of the Town of Richmond.

The choice of polling station was potentially a critical choice in the election outcome. Captain Lyon promoted Richmond while his opponents suggested a location in Fitzroy. Taylor's tavern in Fitzroy won out. But Captains Lyon and Lewis won the election.

Besides the licensed establishments of James Copeland, Mrs. Falls and James McLean, two temperance houses operated during the 1850's in Richmond, hosted by W. Birtch and A. Taylor. The construction of Edward Reilly's new hotel in 1855, set a new standard for public houses that was never again matched.

"The Reilly House"

Edward Reilly was reputed to be Irish to the core - witty, musical and partial to wine, women and song. Employed to take care of the livery and horses at Hugh Bell's hotel in Bell's Corners, he fell in love with the landlords daughter, Sarah. Since his employer would never consent to a match between the two, they eloped. A posse of men hired by Hugh Bell chased the young couple to Perth, where they got married. Eventually father and daughter were reconciled and Hugh Bell assisted his new son-in-law to get started in the hotel business in Richmond.

Being in a central location of a prosperous agricultural area, Richmond had four quarterly cattle fairs each year during the 1850's, 1860's and 1870's. Often the fairs were headquartered at the "Reilly House", where drinking, horse trading, horse racing and more than an occasional fight would occur.

Reilly soon realized the growing demand for accommodation created by the expanding lumber trade in the Upper Ottawa Valley. Richmond was on the main supply road connecting Prescott with the timber cutting areas. Hundreds of sleighs, wagons and teamsters passed through Richmond every fall, winter and spring. He decided that he needed much large premises if he was going to profit from the heavy volume of traffic passing his door. Reilly decided to construct a large stone public house in Richmond in 1855/1856. Open for business in 1857, the "Reilly House" could boast that it was the biggest in the district. For the next twenty years Edward Reilly hosted his public house. Reilly also started a stage coach line which carried mail and passengers between Richmond and Ottawa.

On his death in 1876, his sons Hugh and John took over the proprietorship of the hotel and stage coach businesses, which they successfully ran for the next three decades. The Carleton County Agricultural Society began holding their annual fair at Reilly's in 1896. Today, this historic site including the old "Reilly House" still perform a public function, which has been its role for over 150 years.

A farmer named O'Grady, who attended the Richmond Fair in October 1864, was found dead on the side of the Richmond Road between Richmond and Bell's Corners the next morning. The cause of death was unclear. People who witnessed him leave the Fair, commented on his intoxicated state. It is not clear whether he fell from his horse because of his inebriated condition and sustained injuries which caused his death, or was the victim of foul play.

Adam Hall and Hugh Reilly conducted hotels past 1900 in the Village of Richmond.

Figure 11: "Masonic Arms" tavern in Richmond Ontario. Courtesy of Rideau Twp. Branch of City of Ottawa Archives.

Figure 12: Edward Reilly's Hotel, Richmond, Ontario. Courtesy of Rideau Twp. Branch of City of Ottawa Archives.

BECKWITH TOWNSHIP

Beckwith Township was partially surveyed in 1816, precipitating a small influx of Scottish settlers, followed by a much larger number of Highlanders in 1818.

Prospect

This small hamlet on the Richmond-Perth Road is located in the vicinity of the source of the Jock River, flowing west toward the Rideau. Being located on a busy stage coach route, it became an important stopping place between Perth and Bytown. William Burrows owned and operated the first hotel and post office in the community.

The 1852 Census indicates that James (John) Burrows kept a frame hotel on lot 11, Con. 2 Beckwith at Prospect. John Burrows operated the hotel, store and post office at Prospect together with William Burrows until after 1900.

Franktown

Where the Richmond-Perth military road crossed the upper reaches of the Jock River, the village of Franktown was founded. The military established a supply store midway between Perth and Richmond at Franktown in the fall of 1818. At Franktown, a six hundred acre townsite was laid out by plan of survey in 1819, initially in 25 acre parcels on the Jock River.

Communities began to form such as Franktown on the Old Perth Road. Its location at the crossroads of the north-south road linking Smith Falls with Carlton Place, Ottawa, Almonte, Pakenham and the timber country above Arnprior in Renfrew and Pontiac Counties, placed it along a main commercial travel route.

Former military men, Patrick Nowlan and Thomas Wickham opened public houses in Franktown in 1820. The Journal of Reverend William Bell appears to indicate that Wickham offered more than traditional hospitality to his guests. A Journal entry in 1828 states that Thomas ickham, a Franktown innkeeper appeared in a Perth Court, charged with "keeping a disorderly house and allowing gaming in it."

The first church services were held in the "Franktown Inn", which was not thought to be a suitable environment, so a joint petition was prepared by the various groups of adherents requesting the Lieutenant Governor allow the use of the "King's Store" for worship services for all faiths. This plea was granted. However, the Anglicans commenced the construction of St. James Church within a couple of years, completing it in 1822. It is the oldest Anglican Church in Eastern Ontario still in use.

The overwhelming attitude of the Presbyterian Church and its clergy respecting temperance in the 1820's, 1830's and 1840's, could best be indicated by the fact that Reverend George Buchanan had parishioners who drank regularly with him at the manse in 1825.

As a strategically located crossroads community, Franktown had stage coaches pass stopping with passengers and mail, on the Richmond-Perth Road linking Bytown and Perth and the Brockville – Smith Falls – Pakenham Road. With the anticipation of the Brockville and Ottawa Railway passing through the community, many stores and other businesses established in the hamlet in the early 1850's.

Pioneer innkeeper, Patrick Nowlan in Franktown, accommodated the public between 1820 and 1841. The community hosted two semi-annual Fairs at Patrick Nowlan's public house during the late 1830's and into the 1840's. The 1839 Fair's were held in May and September and were open for horned cattle, horses, hogs, sheep and hawkers.

Ann Burrows and James Burrows took over Nowlan's public house in 1842. Through the 1850's, James Burrows kept the "Franktown Hotel" at the corner of the Concession Road and the intersecting Sideroad in Franktown. Burrows also acted as the Reeve of the Township of Beckwith. He also kept a general store across the road from his public house. Suspected of smuggling, Revenue Officers from Ottawa kept a close watch on him.

Franktown Hotel.

MRS. BURROWS, wishes to inform her friends and the travelling public generally, that she has removed from her old stand to the house formerly occupied by Messrs. J. DRYSDALE & Co. as Store and Post Office. Mrs. B. has fitted up the above house, in a style which will afford both comfort and satisfaction to all who may favour her with their custom. She takes this opportunity of returning her sincere thanks to her Bytown friends and others for the support heretofore received, and assures them that her exertions to please, shall not relax, nor her accommodation be found inferior to any other house of the kind in the country.

Franktown, Dec. 29, 1841.

James Jackson conducted "Jackson's Inn" until 1837 when Peter McGregor leased it and changed the name to the "Franktown Inn". McGregor conducted the house until the late 1840's, when James Jackson, who owned this public house, took over as proprietor again.

Franktown Inn.

THE Subscriber begs to inform the inhabitants of Beckwith, and the public in general that he has rented for a term of years, that well known Tavern stand, formerly called Jacksons' Inn, in Franktown (Beckwith) from the proprietor Mr James Jackson.

He trusts that his prompt and respectful attention to the wishes and comfort of his guests will justify his soliciting a share of public patronage.

An ample supply of WINES & LIQUORS will be kept constantly on hand, and no exertion will be spared to supply his table with the best fare the country can produce. The Stabling is excellent and capacious.

FRANKTOWN INN,

Is in a central part of the country distant 15 miles from Perth, 15 miles from Rich mond, 37 from Bytown, 12 from Smith's Falls, 44 from Brockville 9 from Carleton Place and 42 to the Grand River.

PETER McGREGOR.

Franktown Twp of Beckwith,
June, 8, 1837.

John Hughton opened the third public house, the "Franktown Inn", together with a general store in Franktown by 1850. It reputedly had stabling large enough to hold fifty span of horses. A span of horses comprised four horses, which meant that the outbuildings were large. When Hughton died in 1863, his wife Isabella took over the next year.

Figure 13: John Hughton's Hotel and general store in Franktown, Ont. c. 1865

In 1853, the editor of a Perth newspaper described Franktown:

> *"There has been a great improvement in this place since I visited it last – some ten or twelve years ago. Quite a number of new houses have been erected, and it has quite a village-like appearance.*

The greatest improvement, however, has been made by Mr.
Burrows, who keeps a first-rate hotel. When I was last here, Mr.
Jackson's stone house was the best in the village; but it is now
completely eclipsed by the large and commodious two storey
Hotel erected by Mr. Burrows, and he has finished and
furnished it inside in a style elegant enough to accommodate the
Governor ... " [52]

In the middle fifties, according to Mrs. Atkinson, Franktown was a village of about one hundred and fifty inhabitants, boasting a main street which was a regular beehive of industry, particularly during the lumbering season. Those were the days when the little community was enlivened by the shouts and songs of the rivermen and drivers of supply wagons who stopped there on their way up from Bytown to the McLachlin Brothers shanties. As many as one hundred teams would be seen in the hamlet at one time. During the period when the Brockville and Ottawa railway was being constructed, Franktown district supplied thousands of railway ties. All this industry brought prosperity and busy times to the community. The railway was run within a mile and a quarter of the village.

A peak year for the number of licensed public houses in Franktown was 1863. Joining Andrew Burrows and John Hughton was Thomas Clarke. By 1866, Franktown's population was over 200. Hotels were kept by Thomas Clarke and William Moore in 1866. Another source indicates that Wm. Moore and Thomas Clarke held licenses in Franktown in 1869 - 1872. The Loney family began hotel keeping in the village in 1869 and continued on past the turn of the century. Initially, Elizabeth Loney and then Robert Loney conducted the hotel. Their competition came from William Pierce during the 1880's and beyond 1900.

Beckwith Township residents, James and his son Peter McArthur, operated a distillery using a 33 gallon copper still, from the late 1820's to the 1850's on lot 14, Concession 7, Beckwith. Angus McDonald had a frame tavern on lot 14, Con. 12, Beckwith in 1852.

Figure 14: Hughton's former hotel in Franktown, Ont. in the 1960's with the verandas removed and front door removed.

Figure 15: Former Hughton's Hotel 2007 in Franktown, Ont. Restored and operating as an antique shop in 2007. Photo by Monique Picotte.

Gillies Corners

Gillies Corners on the Perth-Richmond military road, was an important stopping place for teamsters, military personnel and settlers moving into the Bathurst District in the very early days. Being strategically placed at the crossroads in the interior of Eastern Ontario, it had a military and civil importance as a supply route connecting with the Ottawa River at Richmond Landing and the District capital at Perth and Brockville and the lumber districts forming along the Mississippi and Madawaska Rivers. Archibald Gillies had a log tavern on lot 3, Con. 1, Beckwith Twp from the 1830's to the early 1850's.

The community was at an early crossroads which linked Brockville with Smith Falls and the lumber shanties along the Mississippi and Madawaska Rivers. This north-south road took teamsters through Gillies Corners, Carleton Place, Appleton, Almonte, Pakenham to Arnprior. Later a better road would be constructed directly through Franktown to link Smith Falls and Carleton Place, therefore eliminating the north-south traffic through Gillies Corners.

Ashton

Situated partly in the counties of Lanark and Goulbourn Township, Carleton County (now City of Ottawa), the Jock River initially was the focal point of economic activity in the hamlet, with its grist and sawmills.

An early temperance lodge was formed in the hamlet of Ashton in the 1850's. Like many other temperance groups, it gradually died. However, beginning in the mid 1860's the churches started taking a much more active role in the temperance movement, providing organizational and spiritual support to the cause. In particular the Methodists, Baptists and some Presbyterian churches assisted organizations such as the Independent Order of Grand Templars (IOGT) to form several new temples in Beckwith during the late 1860's: Prospect Banner Temple; Ashton Star Lodge organized under Beckwith Reeve James Conn in 1868; Star of Beckwith at Gillies Corners and Maple Grove Lodge at the 7th Line of Beckwith.

For the first time, women were becoming actively involved in the temperance movement, with a few becoming officers in some of the aforementioned temples. Temperance soirees and picnics became popular entertainment venues for many rural communities, notwithstanding the fact that all the attendees did not necessarily support the philosophical position of their hosts.

Donald McFarlane's hotel operated for many years in Ashton beginning in the early 1850's. A local abstemious clergyman described it as "peaceable and quiet house". Two hotels operated in Ashton in 1866-1871 when the population stood at 125 – the "Ashton Hotel" of Daniel Fanning and Donald McFarlane's hotel. Both closed in the early 1890's.

Bad behaviour was sometimes regulated within the community itself.

> *"When there was domestic trouble, they could not repair to a family court. They had their own rough justice for men who neglected their wives and families. The village elders would deputize a strong arm squad to ride the offender on a rail after being tarred and feathered."[53]*

TOWNS AND TAVERNS ALONG THE RIDEAU CANAL

Introduction

Several of the earliest urban settlement areas in Ontario, established along the Rideau Canal. It attracted entrepreneurs who set up sawmills, gristmills, breweries, distilleries, woolen mills and iron foundries, creating an early commercial/industrial corridor. Straddling both sides of the Rideau Canal, communities such as Burritt's Rapids, Merrickville, Smith Falls, Rideau Ferry and Westport, were either located in Lanark County or close enough in proximity, to have strong economic and social linkages.

A Scottish Engineer, John Mactaggart, in charge of the construction of the Rideau Canal, wrote a book about his experiences during the project. He observed that most farmers who were in a suitable location kept tavern, since the license was not high. He stated that when winter roads over river and lake were much easier for travelers, innkeepers frequently "follow with a temporary inn, and there form an establishment on the ice. Sometimes they will remain too long in these inns after the thaw comes on, being greedy and not removing their quarters so long as they are catching a farthing; floods will therefore come on, sometimes during the night, and sweep all to desolation. It is vain for them to anchor the house, as the flakes of ice are sure to cut the cable, even where it chain. Whole families have thus been carried away and drowned; and others brought out of their floating houses alive after drifting many miles down the rivers.

Mactaggart described an adventure that he had with Colonel By and several other officials at a tavern in the wilderness near Bytown, during the construction of the Rideau Canal in 1829.

"All the rooms on the ground floor were crammed full of people of all descriptions; such an ugly, suspicious, dirty-looking set I had never before seen. The slums of Holborn, London, where villains and vagabonds congregate, never were honoured with such a crew .....Potato whiskey and pipes of tobacco seemed in request, and were served out by a bar-maid of such exquisite beauty as Hottentot hath never yet beheld. Not having rested our bones for a long time, fatigue began to overcome us, but there was no place to lie down; as for beds such machines were always perfectly out of the question. A plank, partly clean, was all that could ever be expected in such houses, and indeed over all the semi-civilized part of the country; but in this there was not room to stretch on the floor....Wearied out, the Colonel asked me if I could by any means learn if there were any apartments upstairs. With some trouble the landlord was discovered. This is a difficult thing in an American free and easy, as the host appears so much a guest I succeeded, and having put the question, he guessed there was considerable of room; that I might surmount and see; and if we would kipple up by threes and fours he had buffaloes would kiver us.

Accordingly, the Colonel and a few of our party went up a narrow, frail, dirty staircase; I was afraid of the steps giving way. We then entered a large room, exceedingly cold, round the sides of which a number of weary mortals were stretched. The candle I carried would scarcely burn; for there were frosty windows in the room and few panes of glass in any of them, so that the frosty wind poured in cold and strong. While looking round and muttering to one another, 'This won't do, we shall be frozen to death here', we observed something laid upon an old table and covered with something by way of a sheet. What was this? On removing the same and holding forth the glimmering candle we saw the dead body of a young man, seemingly about fifteen years of age. One side of his head seemed to be mangled in a shocking manner and covered with clotted blood. 'No; this place, indeed, will not do', we all agreed, and downstairs we went. On coming below we found the greater part of the company had 'cleared out', as they say.

Venturing to make some inquiries about the dead lad, we met with nothing by evasive answers – as much as to say it might be better for us to keep a caum saugh – alias, make no noise about it. However, we found this to be impossible; and although some of our party sunk down in sleep on the floor, where melted snow, brought in by the traveler's feet, had flooded, some of us hung on by the wall by the sides of the fire.

In the course of our distant inquiries we found that the greater part of the guests had gone to the barn and the stable, there to kennel up amongst hay; that the dead body upstairs was that of a young Irishman who had been killed two days before by a shot from a gun carelessly let off by one of the sons of the landlord.

In the morning, the father and mother of the lad came crying after us in great tribulation, wishing us to interfere and bring what they called the 'murderer of their dead child' to justice; but this was a thing to us impossible, unless by engaging in an affair we had nothing to do with; and after having done our best, the laws of the country would not probably have exercised then, as we had often seen.....There is something faulty in the administration of the criminal laws, no doubt; but energy and exertion lies dormant in Canada."[54]

William Brennan operated a tavern at the Hogs Back in the Township of Gloucester on the Rideau River, where a public meeting was convened in November 1840. In 1836 the Black Rapids tavern was kept by Hugh Byers.

THE STEAM BOAT
RIDEAU,

WILL leave Kingston for Bytown every Monday, and Bytown for Kingston every Thursday on the arrival of the Steam Boat Shannon. For Freight or Passage apply to the proprietor, ROBERT DRUMMOND.
Kingston, July 10, 1833.

Source: Kingston Chronicle & Gazette, July 13, 1833

Town of Manotick

Two distinctly separate communities comprised present day Manotick. The first community appeared almost instantaneously at the time of the construction of the Rideau Canal. A large labour force of "canallers" appeared about 1828 at "Long Island Locks". The massive construction work in this area employed hundreds of men over several years. Pick and shovel work was slow, laborious and sometimes very dangerous. Deaths from disease, alcohol abuse and fighting were commonplace.

With the establishment of a large work camp in the wilderness, entrepreneurs such as Peter Cameron relocated from Kemptville and set up tavern keeping and a general store in 1829. Soon he added a steamboat service and warehousing and a wharf was added. At the Long Island Locks, Michael Butler operated a general store and hotel during the 1850's and 1860's.

The second community of Manotick, coalesced around the milling operations on the Rideau River and straddled both sides of the waterway.

Being located in parts of four Townships – North Gower, Oxford, Nepean and Goulbourn – created a multiplicity of tavern licensing by-laws and enforcement. This situation certainly benefited the drinking public, but angered the temperance people.

Mill Street was the centre of hotel activity in Manotick in the early days. The "Manotick Hotel" founded by Michael O'Grady was one of the first hostelry's in the business district. O'Grady conducted this public house from 1861 to the early 1870's. Competition during that period came from Johnston McIntyre, who had a hotel nearby and David Kelly (c. 1865 -1872).

By 1864, John Davidson, William Fortune and Thomas Paget also had opened public houses in the community named "Manotick.

Later the "Manotick Hotel" was occupied by Peter Doyle as the "Doyle House" (c.1873) and then "Barney" McCarnen, a colourful Irish wit hosted the public house during the 1880's and 1890's. Years later, Dennis Clarke ran the business as "The Palace" before it burned. The Royal Bank occupies this site in 2007.

In the early 1860's the "Davidson Hotel" of Alexander Davidson operated on Mill Street. He was succeeded by Robert Powell in 1884, who was reputed to have burned down a competitor's hotel later known as the "O'Brien House". Powell operated his hostelry beyond 1900.

James Driscoll established Manotick's fourth hotel in 1876, where a real estate office later stood at 1096 Bridge Street on the east side of the Rideau River. Samuel McEvoy acted as proprietor in the 1880's. After a fire destroyed the hotel, John McCaffrey acquired the lands and constructed the "McCaffrey House" in 1893, which he still operated in 1900.

Figure 16: Davidson Hotel c. 1870, Mill Street, Manotick, Ontario. Courtesy of Rideau Twp. Branch of City of Ottawa Archives.

Figure 17: John McCaffrey constructed this building as the "McCaffrey House" hotelin 1893 at the east end of the bridge across the Rideau River in Manotick, Ontario. Photo by Monique Picotte.

Figure 18: The "Palace Hotel", also known as the "Doyle House" and "Manotick Hotel" when "Barny" McCarnen owned it, stood where the Royal Bank is in Manotick, Ontario. Courtesy of Rideau Township Branch of City of Ottawa Archives.

Village of Kars

The attraction of virgin pine and oak along Stevens Creek near its mouth with the Rideau River attracted several individuals and their families to the vicinity of Kars prior to 1820. Known as "Wellington" until the post office was established in the 1860's, its early growth centred around the sawmill and later the grist mill.

A Loyalist named Richard Garlick settled on lots 28 and 29, Concession 1, North Gower south of Kars about 1821. Garlick hired a crew of shanty men and became heavily involved in the timber trade along the Rideau River and several of its tributaries such as Cranberry Creek. He constructed a stopping place, a school and a crude road to Richmond, as well as the first steam ship on the Rideau River, the "Bytown". Garlick's tavern and wharf was a principal depot for freight, passengers and mail on the steamboat route established in 1829 between Holenback's tavern in Kemptville and Peter Fraser's at Long Island.

Richard Garlick displayed a strong predilection to hard liquor from his earliest arrival. Colonel By's party stopped at his tavern in February 1830, and provided this description:

> "... we came to a Tavern of rather second or perhaps third or fourth rate in the scale of excellence. Here the host was almost unable to speak from the effects of intoxication, but still a person of consequence in the settlement and whose dignity was magnificently displayed in discharging the important duties of path master. The hostess was an active bustling woman who seemed to bear more than her share of the family yoke. Being acquainted with one of our party who had before passed by the same route. In compliment to him the residue of a bottle of wretched brandy was produced, which saved us from the penalty of tasting still more wretched Yankie whiskey. Our stop here of course was limited to but a few minutes, and we again embarked and got under way ... "[55]

Walter Garlick took over the enterprise in the 1850's. Described in one historical document as "unreliable and imbibing too much", Walter

Garlick acquired the same traits of many publicans of the day. He carried on until 1863, when Richard Garlick, his father, was run over by a train while "resting" on the tracks and literally cut in two.

The village of Kars began to take form by the 1850's. Adam J. Eastman started a brewery along the banks of Stevens Creek in the early 1850's in Kars. He produced forty barrels of beer per week. Wanting to attract new residents and businesses, Eastman had a "town plan" surveyed and began selling lots in 1857.

> *"As the river steamers and roads improved, the number of people traveling through the Rideau Valley increased, so that there was a need for a hotel at Kars which could provide more accommodation than that previously supplied by the wharfinger. The "Wellington Hotel" was built by Alexander McEwn in 1858 ... license granted James Selleck ..."* [56]

A store and tavern were kept by Alexander McEwen in Kars in 1857. Business was good so McEwen constructed a larger public house - the "Wellington Hotel" in Kars. James Selleck" hosted it between 1858 and 1863 when Zenas G. Ault assumed its proprietorship from 1864 to 1870. North Gower Township Council held their meetings on a rotational basis at the "Wellington Hotel". Robert Duncan took over in 1878. By 1882, the hotel had been converted to a general store by the new owner, Ira Byce. The building still stands today at the junction of Rideau Valley Drive South and Wellington Streets.

A second hotel appeared along the same street about 1861, constructed by William D. Wood. It was a large two storey frame building comprising twelve bedrooms, a large public dining room, a bar with an entrance from the street and a sample room at the southwest corner. Zenas Ault may have been the proprietor in the mid 1880's. Acquired by John Graham in 1900, the public house underwent a name change to the "Kimberley Hotel". After local option came into effect, the property was utilized as a store until it burned in December 1938. [57]

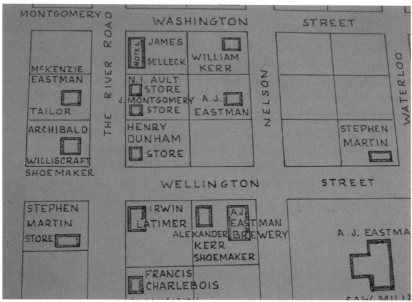

Figure 19: Commercial District of Kars Village c. 1863. Courtesy of Rideau Township Branch of the City of Ottawa Archives.

Figure 20: "Kimberley Hotel", Kars, Ontario c. 1900. Proprietor Jim Graham. Courtesy of Rideau Township Branch of City of Ottawa Archives.

Figure 21: "Wellington Hotel", Kars, Ont., erected c. 1857 by James Selleck. Courtesy of the Rideau Township Branch of the City of Ottawa Archives.

Figure 22: Former "Wellington Hotel" in Kars, Ontario, as it appeared in 2007. Photo by Monique Picotte.

Village of North Gower

Further up Stevens Creek is the community of North Gower. Alternatively, it fell under the jurisdiction of the Districts of Johnstown, Bathurst and finally Dalhousie. The 1851 Census calls it "Stephenville", and indicates that two tavernkeepers resided in the community – Enos Gilbert and Thomas Griffith. Two public houses were located in this milling community in the 1860's– James Johnston's "Union House", which often served as the venue for Council Meetings for the Township of North Gower in the 1860's.

The North Gower Oil Well

During the 1860's, many different business interests were searching for petroleum in Ontario. A group of Canadian and American businessmen assessing the prospects of finding oil in North Gower area in 1865, considered that one location had considerable potential. Excitement ran high as plans were made to drill a deep well. Local publican "Jimmy" Johnston carried out a roaring business hosting drillers and curious visitors by the score in North Gower. But it all turned out to be a hoax, perhaps perpetrated by the hotelkeepers in North Gower. It was discovered that the "oil well" was actually a spring, that parties unknown to the exploration company and villagers, had been liberally "salted" with coal oil each night. The engine and drilling rig pulled out in September 1866, after announcing that "the oil in North Gower was not up to expectations. [58]

· JAS. JOHNSTON'S ·

UNION HOUSE, North Gower. Good Stabling and an attentive Hostler.
January 11 1866.   20-y

Johnston's "Union House" would undergo a number of name changes through the decades. It was known as the "Marlborough House", when James Johnston sold the property in 1886. The new owner, George Ferguson, renamed it the "Ferguson Hotel". By 1895, only George Ferguson retained a license for a "house of public entertainment" in North Gower. The premises burned in 1895, only to be replaced by an even grander structure. When Ferguson sold the premises to Joseph McCurdy in 1907, it became officially known as the "McCurdy House". One hundred years later in 2007, the former "McCurdy House" is still serving beer and food under the name of the Marlborough Pub & Eatery.

William Elliott hosted the community's other public house, "North Gower Exchange Hotel", beginning in the early 1860's. This public house was located just south of the present Rideau Township Archives. J. W. Leach kept this public house in the mid 1880's. When William Gault acted as proprietor of the "Gault House", as it was called in 1893, the old public house burned to the ground, never to rise again.

Presbyterian clergyman, John Gourlay referred to North Gower in his book, "History of the Ottawa Valley" written in 1896:

> *"North Gower was not so much exposed to drink and rowdyism. Its villages were of a much later formation. Education was better attended at an early date ... Men of better principles formed the basis of society, as there were less dregs among the strictly farming classes than where so much promiscuous business was necessarily carried on (ie. Bytown)."*

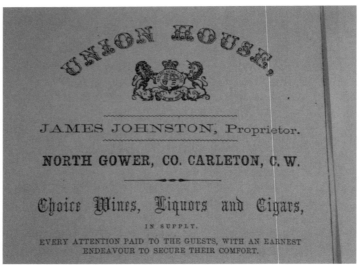

Figure 23: Advertisement for James Johnston's "Union Hotel" which stood where the McCurdy Hotel Building standing in 2007. Source: Mitchell's Commercial Directory, 1864.

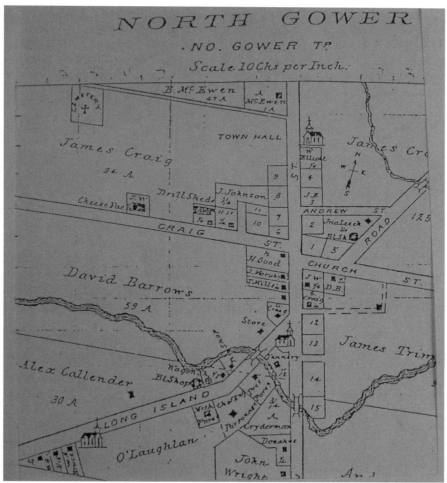

Figure 24: Map of the Village of North Gower, Ontario. Note the "Long Island Road" linking Manotick with Beckett's Landing and Burritt's Rapids, through Pierce's Corners.

Figure 25: "McCurdy House" c.1896, erected on the site of the previous "Union House". Today this building functions as the village of North Gower "pub". Courtesy of the Rideau Township Branch of City of Ottawa Archives.

Pierce's Corners

A small community appeared at this location at the junction of the Long Island Road linking Manotick with North Gower and Burritt's Rapids and the north – south Malakoff Road connecting Richmond with Alexander Beckett's Landing. A ferry service across the Rideau River linked travelers with Kemptville.

John Pierce settled on the west half of lot 6, Concession 5, Marlborough in the 1820's. Steven's Creek ran across the property, which he utilized to operate a sawmill and to engage in lumbering.

John Pierce erected a three storey log hotel of square timber circa 1843, facing onto the Malakoff Road (which at that time was called the "Richmond Road"). One half of the second storey was a ballroom; the third floor sleeping quarters. John Gourlay, a staunch Presbyterian clergyman commented that "at the corners from early days, the Pierces kept a very respectable stopping place." Marlborough Township Council often met there until the new Town Hall was constructed at Pierces Corners in 1855. Pierce became actively involved in the political life of Marlborough, serving as Reeve of the Municipality.

An old veteran of the British Army, David Harbison, was a frequent customer at Pierces tavern – in fact he might have been described as a "fixture". Anyways, he happened to be John Pierce's brother-in-law. But what made the old government pensioner unique was his wooden leg, acquired after partaking in a battle in which his original limb went astray. It was during an election held at Pierce's tavern, during the days of the "open ballot", when an elector verbally told the returning officer, who he cast his ballot for that Harbison gained additional fame. Apparently, his support for a certain candidate did not please the large crowd gathered in the barroom to witness the voting. Hisses and cat calls were hurled in the direction of the old soldier. These insults were quickly replaced by verbal threats and shoving. Harbison was backed into a corner by a drunken, hostile mob, which was now on its unsteady feet – and demanding blood. Backed into a corner by the mob, Harbison unstrapped his wooden leg and used it successfully to defend both himself and his political convictions.

Another story related to Pierce's tavern involved an old tippler who would come in for "just one drink", but couldn't seem to leave the place. Often his wife would arrive at the tavern in a fury, looking for him. If she found him, he was liable to receive more than a "verbal" tongue lashing. The patrons took pity on his plight. The boys in the barroom decided that a signal would be given upon the approach of the angry woman, which enabled her husband enough time to scramble out a tavern window.

After the death of John Pierce in 1851, his widow Rebecca hosted the tavern for a few years, until her twin sons James and John were able to assume the proprietorship for awhile. These boys were referred to as "giants" because of their large size. The twins' tavern was first on the north-west corner, owned by James, but after a fire it was rebuilt on John's land opposite. The tavern was well known for "food as good as it was plain, for being as comfortable as it was clean, and for being as orderly as two giants could keep it."

Later Robert Kerr operated the hotel and general store in the mid 1860's before acquiring a hotel in Kemptville. James Pierce acted as innkeeper in the late 1860's and into the 1870's. Eventually, the old stopping place was converted into a residence, after the top storey of the building was removed. It still stands today in a much modified state. James Pierce sold a lot off his farm holding on the north-west corner of the crossroads to John Henderson, who erected a hotel.

By 1880, Pierces Corners performed a wide variety of important public functions in Marlborough Township. Its central location and good access encouraged the erection of an Anglican Church, Orange Hall, Town Hall, school house, Odd Fellows Hall and two taverns.

Figure 26: John Pierce erected this log "hotel" complete with a second floor "ballroom" in 1843. The tavern served as a Colonial meeting place for Marlborough Council in the 1840's and early 1850's at Pierece's Corners, Ont. Courtesy of Rideau Township Branch of City of Ottawa Archives.

Town of Kemptville

Sometimes referred to as the "south branch of the Rideau River", Kemptville Creek flows northward into the Rideau River out of northern Grenville County. The initial settlement area occurred on the north shore of Kemptville Creek. The future town site formed around the sawmill, grist mill and distilleries located along the banks of this stream course.

Peter Fraser established an early tavern near the mill site in 1827 on the south side of Clothier Street. James Adams opened his inn nearby in 1828.

The Clothier family played a dynamic role in the development of the early hamlet. Lyman Clothier performed the role of Town Clerk for Oxford

Township in 1829. The family also constructed a sawmill, gristmill and a public house to accommodate the farmers utilizing their milling services.

The importance of early taverns for providing a place for public functions was shown by the fact that the first Catholic Mass in Kemptville "was celebrated in Asa Clothier's log hotel" in the late 1820's. Clothier sold his hotel to Nathan R. Hollenback about 1828. Oxford Township Council met at this public house in the early 1830's.[59]

> During the construction of the Rideau Canal, a steamship began
> running in April 1829, linking the Village of Kemptville and the
> "head of Long Island", later known as Manotick. A notice
> placed in the Brockville Record newspaper in the spring of 1830
> by innkeepers Nathan Holenbeck, Peter Fraser and Richard
> Garlick announced the venture thusly: "... to inform the public,
> that there will be a regular line of conveyance established ...
> during the ensuing season, from the Village of Kemptville to the
> head of Long Island. ... Boats will be in readiness to convey
> passengers each morning of the week from Nathan P.
> Holenbeck's Inn of Kemptville, to the head of Long Island or
> from Peter Fraser's Inn at the head of Long Island ..."[60]

The name of Nathan Holenbeck's tavern – the "Freemasons' Arms" – c. 1828, indicates that Freemasonry was present in the community at an early time.

A commercial boom occurred in Kemptville in 1830, when the first steamboat appeared on the South Branch of the Rideau River (Kemptville Creek). The community was now linked with the outside world and its markets by the miracles of the construction of the Rideau Canal and the invention of the steam engine. Soon wharves appeared on both sides of the Kemptville Creek at the bridge as products such as potash could now be easily shipped to the Montreal market and manufactured goods brought into the area.

Discussions about forming a temperance society in Kemptville in 1830 were mentioned in a Brockville newspaper. This indicates that there was a serious concern amongst a segment of the community's population related to the proliferation of groggeries and the attendant drunkenness.

Several other public houses appeared in Kemptville in the late 1820's and early 1830's. James Adam's tavern was in business as early as 1826. A public meeting of the landowners and other inhabitants of the Townships of Oxford, Marlborough, North and South Gower, was convened in front of Mr. Adam's Hotel at Kemptville in October 1831. The number of residents that appeared at the meeting was too large to be accommodated in the tavern. Peter Fraser established a tavern on the south side of Clothier Street east of West Street c. 1826.

Increased commerce and population growth led to the construction of more public houses in Kemptville. Abram Beach established an inn at the north end of Prescott Street c. 1831. Mahlon Beach opened a small frame hotel on the northwest corner of Clothier and West Streets in 1832. This hotel was soon acquired by brewer Thomas Beckett in 1833 and William McGregor in the late 1840's.

A correspondent passing through the community in the fall of 1831 described the village having an Anglican Church, Methodist Chapel, three taverns, two merchant shops and saw, grist and carding mills.

Coleman's Inn hosted an organizational meeting of area Reformers in January 1834, preparing for a general election held that year.

Nathaniel Fenton constructed the "White House" about 1835 at the corner of Prescott and Clothier Streets. After a few years he sold it to Thomas Adams, who operated it from the 1840's to the 1870's. Fenton then erected a stone building on the corner of Clothier and North Rideau Streets, which he operated as a hotel.

The "King William III Hotel" opened about 1842 in a converted building. Its proprietors in succession were Alexander Beckett, Thomas Johnston, William Johnston and Robert Kerr in the late 1860's and 1870's when it was known as the "Kerr House".

Thomas Beckett, an enterprising young man entered the life of a publican in 1833. His tavern was the site of a Government auction conducted to sell Clergy Reserve Lands in October 1833. He also kept a store and in 1837 established a brewery on Kemptville Creek west of Clothier's mill.

Thomas Beckett's "Kemptville Brewery" manufactured beer to supply the numerous taverns in the area well into the 1860's.

THE STEAMER

CLOTHIER.

THE Proprietors have much pleasure in announcing to the Public that their fast sailing Steamer, the CLOTHIER, will be ready to commence her regular trips between

KEMPTVILLE & BYTOWN,

On MONDAY, second of May next.

The CLOTHIER will leave Kemptville on the mornings of Monday, Wednesday and Friday, at 9 o'clock, A. M.; and Bytown on the mornings of Tuesday, Thursday and Saturday, at 5 o'clock, A. M., arriving at Kemptville in time to enable the Passengers to reach Prescott by stage the same evening.

By this pleasant and expeditious route passengers will be conveyed from Bytown to Kingston in the short period of

ONE AND A HALF DAYS.

To such as feel disposed to test the virtues of the celebrated CALEDONIA SPRINGS, this route offers peculiar facilities, being decidedly the most agreeable as well as the nearest course from the upper part of the Province and neighbouring States.

The Proprietors trust their exertions for the convenience and comfort of the Travelling Community will be such as to merit that patronage which they now respectfully solicit.

LYMAN CLOTHIER, & Co.

Kemptville, 2d April, 1842.

Alexander Beckett owned the wharf on the Rideau known as "Beckett's Landing" where larger steamboats stopped when visiting Kemptville in 1830's and 1840's. He also conducted a ferry service across the Rideau River for road travelers between Richmond and Kemptville. This is where the Governor General Charles Poulett Thomson (Lord Sydenham) stopped during a visit in October 1840. He also acquired a hotel in Kemptville, which he ran for many years.

William McGregor acquired Thomas Beckett's old hotel in the late 1840's and soon tore it down. He replaced it with the new "American House Hotel". His public house became one of the most respectable hotels in the Kemptville area. McGregor was a very active member of the Mt. Zion Masonic Lodge, which held its meetings at his hotel from 1855 to 1858. For over twenty-five years, the "American Hotel" and its host William McGregor, were prominent parts of the Kemptville business community. The building was destroyed by fire in 1991.

Merchant Joseph Bower began a distillery in Kemptville in 1847, employing William McGregor as his distiller. During the 1850's, George Ross worked as his distiller. Bower also acted as village treasurer and school trustee.

Ambrose Clothier operated a distillery, general store and sawmills in the Village in the 1840's and 1850's. Lyman Clothier ran a hotel during the same time period, as did Henry Perkins and his widow in the 1850's.

During the 1850's, Kemptville was home to five or six public houses on an annual basis. As the number of trades people and industry grew in the community, Kemptville's trade area continued to expand further into the countryside. The growth of the surrounding farm economy strongly supported the growth of the Village. In 1857, the community separated from the Township of Oxford and became an incorporated "Village" under the Municipal Act.

Five hotels vied for patronage in Kemptville during the early 1860's. Three of these public houses were on Clothier Street. William Johnston hosted the "King William III Hotel"; Thomas Adams, the "Adam's Hotel"; John Sellick operated the "Sellick Hotel" on Prescott Street; William McGregor hosted the "American House"; the "Kemptville Hotel"; the "Rideau House"; Mrs. Hyndman, 1864;

Three Constables maintained law and order in the community in the early 1860's: Michael Keenan; T. Allan; William Banks and Robert Dougall.

William Burrill's appearance as an hotel keeper in Kemptville happened about 1870. For the next decade he served a prominent role as a leading publican in the community. Other hostelry's of note during that time period were the "Farmer's Hotel" operated by Robert Kerr 1868 – 1893;

"Adam's Hotel" of Thomas Adams; the "American House" of William McGregor 1848 – 1875; John Sellick's "Sellick's Hotel", 1865-1871;

An old man in Kemptville named William Magee was found dead in his bed in which state the body had lain a considerable time without any information being given to the neighbours of the occurrence. The deceased's wife was suspected and Coroner's Inquest was held, when it was found that the deceased and his wife had quarreled in their "cups" and that in self defence the wife had been the cause of her husbands death. Mrs. Mageee was lodged in the Brockville gaol to await trial.[61]

A tornado hit downtown Kemptville in June 1874 and caused a considerable amount of damage to the community's public houses. In a couple of minutes, the roofs on Robert Kerr's sheds and barns, as well as William McGregor's hotel and barns, were torn off. Thomas Adam's hotel suffered extensive damage as well.[62]

During the 1880's and 1890's1886-1887, Burrill House: 1892-93 host G. Lucas; "Central House", Thomas Warren 1884 to 1894; Farmer's Hotel of Robert Kerr 1884 to 1898. T.M. Garland 1892-1894; McPherson House proprietor George McPherson 1892-1894 advertised his "first class Sample Rooms for Commercial Travellers. The bar is supplied with the Best Brands of Cigars and Liquors."

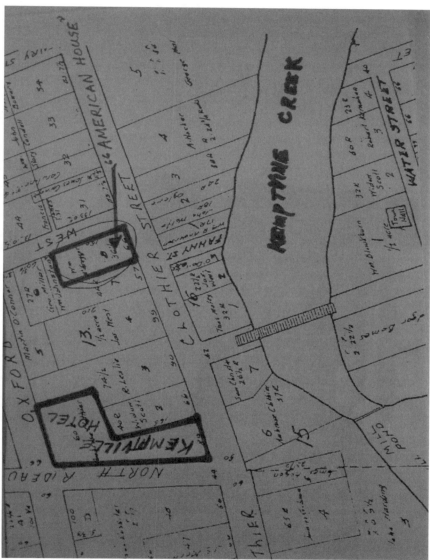

Figure 27: Hotel Locations in Kemptville, Ont.c. 1865

Figure 28: "Burrill House" was a prominent hostelry in Kemptville, Ontario run by William Burrell between 1870 and 1888. Source: "Pioneer Inns and Taverns Vol. 2" by Edwin C. Guillett

Figure 29: "Kemptville Hotel" at corner of North Rideau and Clothier Streets, Kemptville, Ont. c. 1965

Figure 30: "American House", Kemptville, Ont. Erected 1847. Courtesy of Bonnie Paul.

Oxford Mills

Also located on the banks of Kemptville Creek, Oxford Mills began as an early mill site. Asa Clothier constructed a grist mill utilizing a log dam across the South Branch of the Rideau River. The need for accommodation for farmers visiting the mill from a distance, led to the erection of "Clothier's Hotel" c. 1835. About twenty years later the hostelry sold to William Marvin in 1853. Other proprietors over the next few decades were William Kelly; Alexander Gibson; John McPherson ; Joseph Todd; William Alexander; Mary Alexander; Thomas McLean; James Leach; William Leach; Thomas Warren. It stood vacant in 2007.

A public meeting of the freeholders in the Townships of Montague, Oxford, Marlborough and Wolford was held in September 1834 at Adam's Inn in Oxford Mills.

Irishman, Archibald McGee kept a popular stopping place along Kemptville Creek in Oxford Mills from the early 1850's into the late 1860's. Situated on Water Street just north of Clothier's Hotel, McGee's public house served a number of important community functions. The

Council of the Township of Oxford held their meetings on the premises in the 1850's and 1860's. The adherents of the Anglican Church conducted services upstairs until 1869, when they built a church.

Innkeepers in 1865 were Archibald McGee and Henry Anderson. George Henry "Yankie" Davis hosted the third hotel along a stretch of Water Street from the mid 1860's and into the 1870's. This building which later served as a bakery now is a residential structure in 2007. By 1871, a 44 year old Irishman, John Davis operated a hotel in Oxford Mills in direct competition with "Yankie Davis". James Johnston kept the third hotel in Oxford Mills in 1871.

Clothier's hotel functioned in Oxford Mills during the 1880's- 1890's with different proprietors: 1886-1887, J. Sanderson; 1892-93 Mrs. James Alexander;1894, L.Willis; W. J. Leach, 1895 to 1900.

Figure 31: Former "Clothier's Hotel" c. 1835, Oxford Mills, Ont. Farmers bringing grain to the grist mill on the South Branch of the Rideau River, frequented this inn for decades. Photo by Monique Picotte.

Figure 32: Former the hotel of George "Yankie" Davis on Water St., Oxford Mills, Ont. One of three public along the west side of Water St. backing onto the South Branch of the Rideau River. It is now a private residence. Photo by Monique Picotte

Figure 33: "Archie" McGee's Hotel, Oxford Mills, Ont. Oxford Township Council often met here in the 1860's. Local Anglican's held worship services on the second floor until building a church in 1869.

Bishop's Mills

A third community located on the South Branch of the Rideau River, Bishop's Mills, boasted of the tavern of Andrew Kirkland, who operated it in the late 1850's. William McLennan kept this house during the 1860's and into the early 1870's. James McLees operated a public house in Bishop's Mills in the 1880's and 1890's, closing the premises about 1898. Mrs. E. Baker remained open until 1894.

North Augusta

A fourth hamlet on the South Branch maintained two public houses during the 1850's, 1860's and 1870's. The "Victoria House", H.H. Bellamy, 1865,1869; "North Augusta Hotel" of Wm. Humphries, 1857, 1865, 1869; 1871 James Wight and James Aspinall

The "Union Hotel" hosted by John B. Davis was the last hotel to operate in the community. He conducted it during the 1880's and into the late 1890's. His competitor, John L. Joynt hosted the "Victoria House" until the turn of the century.

Oxford Station

A station on the St. Lawrence & Ottawa Railway had a hotel run by Andrew Holmes, who also acted as postmaster in 1871.

Burritt's Rapids

It straddles the two Townships of Marlborough (now City of Ottawa) and Oxford. Originally settled because of the ample water power available on the Rideau River, it began its life as a lumbering centre for the Rideau River hinterland.

Richard Olmstead, who settled on lot 19, Concession 1, Marlborough Township, conducted the first tavern in Burritt's Rapids starting about 1796. Olmstead's log tavern was located just east of the narrow canal bridge at Burritt's Rapids in Oxford Township. This public house had the distinction of being the very first tavern in Carleton County or the City of Ottawa as it is now known. The first Town Meeting, which appointed various municipal officials, was held at this public house in 1823. It served as the Township Hall until 1842. When Marlborough and North Gower Townships became part of the Dalhousie District, the Township meetings transferred to a more central locale – Pierce's Corners or Malakoff as it was sometimes called.

About that time his son Rufus Olmstead took over. He moved the tavern business to larger premises, a stone building on lot 20, Marlborough Township. This location was adjacent to Beckett's Landing, where riverboats stopped with passengers and freight for Richmond and Kemptville.

The quality of these early stopping places varied considerably from landlord to landlord. An early traveler journeying from Bytown (Ottawa) to Kingston in 1830 described his impressions of the inn that he stayed at in Burritt's Rapids thusly:

> *"Here the accumulation of filth and dirt was too much for light*
> *spirits like ours to endure. We had been enured to comfort and*
> *cleanliness, the last we considered within the reach of all*
> *however poor. But the stench which here arose from filth, from*
> *fat and from uncleanliness of every sort beggars description.*
> *Around the table overlaid with the accumulated slops and*
> *grease of many a fowl but fat feasts sat a parcel of lazy looking,*
> *uncouth haggard beings, the picture of indolence and slouth .....*
> *the juvenile maidens attending around were plentifully*
> *besmeared with the oil and rancid butter..... There was however*
> *one, a noted youth above the rest, in whom some latent spark of*
> *rude politeness was struggling to break forth amid the rudeness*
> *of Yankee vulgarity which overwhelmed it."[63]*

The building of the Rideau Canal by Colonel By from 1827 to 1832, had a profound impact on the growth and development of Burritt's Rapids. A dam and lock constructed at Burritts Rapids, employed several hundred men headed by a company of Royal engineers. Superb craftsmen in working with stone and wood, were recruited for the project and left their legacy in the numerous heritage stone and frame buildings in the vicinity of the community. They stayed in the hamlet, creating demand for additional accommodation and numerous other services. It also acted as a supply depot for the construction crews working on the Canal in the more remote areas. The hamlet grew larger and prospered. The erection of a grist mill in 1831, together with saw and shingle mills, attracted considerable commerce to the village.

After the completion of the Canal, the community became an important transportation centre for commercial traffic on the waterway.

"About mid-century, substantial hotels were erected in the Rideau Corridor, a move reflecting the commercial development of the period. These buildings followed no fixed style or design and were constructed of frame, brick or stone. One early frame hotel in Burritt's Rapids with full width upper galleries existed until 1971." [64]

Abel Adams hosted another early public house located on the west half of lot 6, Concession 1, Oxford Township. His premises carried the distinction of hosting the first meeting of Free Masons in the area, which inaugurated Rideau Lodge No. 25 of the Eastern District. As the era of simple log taverns was eclipsed by larger and more refined "hotels", old stands such Adam's tavern faded into obscurity.

In 1851, the Census indicates that three public houses existed in Burritt's Rapids. They were conducted by John Healy, John McKerrigan and Thomas Johnston.

Thomas Johnston's frame tavern in Burritt's Rapids was described in 1851 thusly: "travelers will find a good house and the charges are moderate." Business prospered and Johnston erected a frame tavern in 1857, just north of the narrow bridge entrance crossing the Rideau on Grenville Street. This public house boasted every publicans dream – a ballroom. After Johnston's death in 1857, William Read took over as proprietor of the "Commercial Hotel" in 1861 to 1865; perhaps Noble Johnston operated it 1866-1870; James Johnston, 1871. Mrs. Fanny Johnston may have been the proprietor in the mid 1880's, while Charlie White inhabited it later. The old landmark burned in 1970.

Ironically, years of brawling and drunken rowdiness failed to produce the violence which occurred after the hotel ceased to function as a public house. After prohibition closed the hotel down, it was converted into two residential dwellings. During the 1920's the two residents – Walter Percival and his next door neighbour, O'Shea, got into an argument over a trivial matter. Returning from church one Sunday, O'Shea decided to fill his wood box up in the house. While carrying wood from the rear shed, he left the gate open to ease the task. When his neighbour Percival ordered him to close the gate, O'Shea refused. A very angry Percival returned into his house and retrieved a gun. Proceeding back outside, he confronted O'Shea and during the ensuing argument, Percival shot O'Shea in the head, killing him. Percival served a year in penitentiary for the crime.

Thomas Brown operated a tavern on the south side of the river in Oxford Township, just west of the "T" intersection at the River Road and the main street of Burritt's Rapids in the mid 1850's. Brown died in 1867, but his widow continued to act as proprietor into the early 1870's. This old log hostelry stood immediately east of the stone house on the south side of the canal.

Uriah Depencier hosted the frame "North Burritts Rapids Hotel" across the road from the Anglican Christ Church throughout most of the 1850's; H. J. Rickey acquired the property from Depencier c. 1861 and various proprietors conducted the business. This historical building still stands in the community today.

A fourth hotel in Burritt's Rapids during part of the 1850's and 1860's was kept by a number of proprietors: Frederick A. Moore, 1854; William Kidd, 1857; Daniel O'Neil, 1861.

ATTEMPTED MURDER

Daniel McCullough went to Burritt's Rapids in the fall of 1862, to pick up money owed to him. Stopping at William Read's hotel, he was approached by a man named James Ward, who requested a ride to Kemptville. McCullough agreed to give the stranger a lift. After taking a few glasses of whiskey, they left together.

Within a few miles of Kemptville, Ward stopped the horse and taking out a knife, demanded that McCullough five him his money. At the same time Ward remarked, that he made his living murdering men. Seizing McCullough by the coat with one hand and with the other drew a knife several times across McCullough's throat. He then let go his hold, knocked him down and commenced kicking him until he supposed the farmer was dead. After this was accomplished, he jumped back into his victim's cutter, turned the horse around and drove furiously until he reached Merrickville. Stopping at Crozier's tavern in Merrickville, Ward fortified himself with several glasses of whiskey and then left for Easton's Corners leaving the stolen cutter behind.

Meanwhile, a badly injured McCullough, was found along the roadside by William Read, the hotelkeeper from Burritt's Rapids. Recognizing McCullough, he lifted him into his sleigh and took the injured man to a doctor in Kemptville. McCullough was able to identify his attacker to the authorities.

Michael Keenan, a Constable from Kemptville, together with Special Constable James Walmsley, pursued Ward to Merrickville. Learning that the fugitive had stopped at Roger Crozier's tavern, they determined that he was fleeing to the west. Ward rode west to Easton's Corners, unaware that the authorities were close behind. The lawmen caught up to the fugitive, who attempted to escape on foot, but couldn't evade capture.

At his trial, James Ward was convicted of attempted murder and sentenced to be hung in July 1863, notwithstanding the fact that Daniel McCullough recovered from his wounds. The twenty-four year old Ward had just been released from Federal Penitentiary, where he served a term of three years. [65]

Between the 1860's and the late 1880's, three public houses continued to operate in Burritt's Rapids. The northern part of the community was served by "Rickey's Hotel", while Stephen Collins operated the "Union House Hotel" in 1868 - 1871 and Mrs. Fanny Johnston conducted the "Commercial Hotel", respectively. Mrs. Johnston ceased operating 1890.

By 1871, Burritts Rapids boasted a population of 400 people, with two sawmills, two shingle mills, a grist mill and a carding and fulling mill.

Throughout the 1880's and after 1900, Daniel O'Neil and Hezekiah Rickey, hosted their respective public houses in Burritt's Rapids.

Figure 34: "North Burritt's Rapids Hotel" c. 1850. Erected by Uriah De Pencier, who acted as landlord until early 1860's when Hezekiah Rickey took over, conducting it as "Rickey's Hotel" until c. 1900.

Figure 35: "Commercial Hotel" c. 1847, originally conducted by Thomas Johnston 1848 to 1857; then William Reid until mid 1860's. It burned in 1970.

Village of Merrickville

Merrickville encompasses lands on both sides of the Rideau waterway – the north side lies in Montague Township, Lanark County, while the south side is in Wolford Township, Grenville County.

By 1820, Merrickville was reputedly the largest urban centre on the whole Rideau waterway. "Merrick's Mills" comprised saw and grist mills, a general store, a blacksmith's shop, a couple of taverns, and a storehouse, together with several private dwellings. An early tavern in the hamlet was Huffman's Inn during the 1831-1833 period.

Still standing on the north side of the Rideau Canal near the bridge, a small stone "cottage" erected in the late 1820's, is reputed to have been a tavern in the early days of the community. The "Merrick Tavern" situated on the north side of the Canal opposite the Blockhouse, was constructed about 1830 to accommodate the workers employed in the construction project and for the workers employed in the industrial complex across the street. The owners of the small stone building, which still stands beside the waterway at 106 Mill Street, were Aaron and Terrance Merrick.

The same traveler on his way to Kingston in 1830, who stopped at a tavern in nearby Burritt's Rapids, spent the next evening at Turner's Inn at Merrickville. His impression of this stopping place seemed to be more positive:

> *"The beds in their leaving here were clean but rather poor and scanty in their longitude. The pillows, or rather the apology for pillows, bear a nearer resemblance to pancakes that the purpose for which they were intended .... The viands were good and served up with due attention to cleanliness so that with the assistance of the traveler to warm up the plates, a tolerably comfortable meal can be had here....*"[66]

A distillery located north of the locks on the Rideau Canal was operational in 1831.[67]

"Penny A Day Men"

Regular British Army troops were stationed at the blockhouse in Merrickville from time of the construction of the Canal in the area in 1829. Security from an American attack was the principal reason for their presence, although maintaining law and order amongst the troublesome work force, occupied their time and attention initially.

These troops were poorly paid by anyone's standards of the day. However, the British Government utilized a strategy to keep the troops happy and build an esprit de corp – it provided them with booze! Each man was allocated a daily ration of beer – actually five beer to be exact. The ration took the form of "beer money" because the soldiers received a penny a day, which could buy them five pints or some equivalent in whiskey or other "ardent spirits". Each night the Merrickville taverns hosted their "protectors" and helped them spend their "ration" money.

This practice by the British military authorities was in part, considered important for the physical and mental health of its troops. It certainly enlivened the evening proceedings throughout the numerous inns around the area.

The degree of industrial development in Merrickville present at the time of the opening of the Rideau Canal is perhaps exemplified by property sales. In January 1833, a large and commodious dwelling house, a distillery, a potash factory, stables and sheds, near the locks and sawmills and grist mills of Mr. Merrick was offered for sale in a Brockville newspaper.

Area residents who supported Reformer candidates, gathered for an organizational meeting in January 1834 at Olmstead's Inn at Merrickville. By 1840, the population of Merrickville passed 900 people.

The 1851 Census indicates that Samuel Robinson and "Robert"Crozier kept public houses in the Village. It was at Crozier's Hotel that the suspected murder fugitive, James Ward, rested while fleeing from his attempt to murder Daniel McCullough in 1862. Innkeeper Crozier also played a part in a riot that occurred on the Main Street of Merrickville in the summer of 1861. Crozier's hotel and nine other buildings were destroyed by fire caused by a spark from the blacksmith's shop in August 1864.[68]

Tavern licensing was a significant source of income to municipalities. The cost of license could vary greatly, from Township to Township. In 1854, John Burrows and Stephen Merrick operated taverns in the Montague portion of North Merrickville. Complaints by the two innkeepers to Council about the high cost for a license for public entertainment, fell on deaf ears. Burrows relocated his tavern business to the south side of the Rideau River in the Wolford Township section of Merrickville in the spring of 1855.

Merrickville was by-passed by the Brockville & Ottawa Railway in 1858, which traveled through Smith Falls. In fact the community was not successful in obtaining a branch line to Smith Falls either. Ironically, Merrickville's population, ten years after the railway arrived in nearby Smith Falls, was still the same as its rival. The economic and population benefits of having a railway, did not seem to matter in the 1860's in Lanark County.

The "City Hotel" on St. Lawrence Street dates back to the early 1850's. Hosted by James Armstrong from 1855, the first Council meeting for the newly incorporated Village of Merrickville occurred there in July 1860. James Armstrong was the proprietor until about 1885 when Michael Fitzgerald took over in 1894. Almost doubled in size in 1902, by proprietor J. A. McCabe, the "City Hotel", later was known as the "Grenville Hotel" and the "Goose and Grid Iron".

In the latter part of the 1850's, William Fortune acted as the proprietor of the "Rideau Hotel" in Merrickville, while William Kelly had "Kelly's Hotel".

During the early 1860's, James Eagleton conducted the "Exchange Hotel" on Main Street, but the most astonishing fact is that 92 year old Mary Eagleton is listed as the proprietor of this public house in the 1871 Census.

The "Merrickville Hotel" on St. Lawrence Street was hosted by the McIntyre family for three decades. Initially, Daniel McInyyre held the license in the 1860's, followed by Bridget McIntyre from 1871 to about 1880.

The Merrick family kept the "North Merrickville Hotel" on the north side of the Canal from 1830 until the late 1860's. Stephen Merrick acted as the principal innkeeper. Its location beside the locks and across the Canal from the military blockhouse, where it still stands today, made it a popular rendezvous and stopping place.

In the 1860's, James M. Robison operated a saloon on St. Lawrence Street. The "Union House" was occupied by J. D. Stark, 1864; E. N. Southworth, 1865/66. Diamond & Jordan were hotelkeepers in Merrickville in 1864 and also were general merchants and liquor dealers.

A temperance society was formed in Merrickville in 1830, modeled after the nearby Bastard Township Temperance Society. It promoted the exaggerated claim that when it was organized, more than 15,000 gallons of whiskey were manufactured annually in Bastard Township.

These early societies did not call for abstinence from alcohol consumption – merely moderation. The Good Templars, a temperance organization, had a Hall where they conducted their meetings in May 1862.

𝔇𝔦𝔰𝔤𝔯𝔞𝔠𝔢𝔣𝔲𝔩 𝔄𝔰𝔰𝔞𝔲𝔩𝔱 𝔬𝔫 𝔞 𝔐𝔢𝔪𝔟𝔢𝔯 𝔬𝔣 𝔭𝔞𝔯𝔩𝔦𝔞𝔪𝔢𝔫𝔱

During the Provincial election campaign in the summer of 1861, Francis Jones, member of Parliament for the South Riding of Leeds and Grenville, was electioneering in the village of Merrickville. During one of his speeches, Jones alluded to some of the tactics that his opponents were employing to defeat him. Jones stated that his enemies had tried cultivators and plough points and even resorted to a dash of holy water. Patrick Dowdie, an Irish Catholic, who also happened to be Bailiff of the County Division Court, considered the comments of Jones, a slight against his creed and vowed revenge.

The next day, as Jones was walking with a friend through the business district of downtown Merrickville, Dowdie heading up a mob of about 40 men, accosted Jones.

Dowdie dashed a pail of water in Jones face and aided by a number of other men, knocked him down, and proceeded to handle him very roughly. While matters remained in this state, Jones drew a loaded revolver to protect himself, but before he could use it this was taken from him and broken. Mr. Crozier, a tavern keeper, rushed to the assistance of the

M.P.P. and was also knocked down by some of Dowdie's gang and very much severely injured. In the number of his assailants Mr. Jones found comparative safety and finally escaped without receiving really serious injuries. Jones attempted to prosecute Dowdie and the other leaders of the riot, but failed to gain any convictions. Such was the state of law and order in Eastern Ontario in 1861. [69]

The "Five Gallon" Men

The regulation of the sale of alcohol outside of "houses of public entertainment" or taverns as they were colloquially known, before 1853 was a rather haphazard affair. The Temperance Act of 1853 attempted to improve the management of liquor sales from stores and other outlets holding "shop licenses". Any business carrying a few items of foodstuffs could by licensed to sell liquor off the shelves or "small" samples on the premises. be

It was common practice at stores to keep a barrel of "high wines" or whiskey at the back, which regular customers customers were free to sample at will. The store owners considered it good business to "treat" customers, which in turn would put them in the mood to more freely purchase items. While the drink(s) were free to all who came in, it was assumed that only people intending to be customers would take advantage of the hospitality offered.

Drinks were secured by the use of a tin dipper attached to a string. Everyone drank from the same vessel. Virtually every merchant and tradesman, from the blacksmith to the clothing store, had a large keg of whiskey on the premises to humour their customers. Custom dictated that any customer wanting to have several "sips" would pay a small tariff – for instance a "grunt" – meaning all you could drink without taking a breath, cost a penny. Good customers would gather in groups around the whiskey barrel at the back of store and sip, while gossiping.

This practice together with allowing sales of whiskey off the shelf in quart jars, was considered by the temperance people to be a major cause of public drunkenness witnessed on the Village streets. When the "Dunkin

Act" was passed in 1864, it attempted to control the dispensing of booze through "shop licenses" by requiring vendors to sell whiskey or beer in minimum amounts of five gallons or a dozen bottles per customer.

Instead of controlling the inebriation of "shoppers", bulk purchases had the opposite effect. On market day in Merrickville, Richmond, Kemptville, Manotick and Burritt's Rapids, the sidewalks and streets were crowded with drunken, reeling customers. Each man wanting to "treat" his friends and acquaintances and in turn be treated, drinking freely, while his spouse did the real shopping. Thus the term "five gallon men" came about.

During the 1880's and 1890's, Merrickville prospered from its industrial enterprises and Canal traffic. One popular public house during this time as the "Windsor Hotel" hosted by Josiah Payne – 1884 to 1893. When the proprietorship went to W.M. Ross in 1894, he boasted that the "Hotel is beautifully situated on the Rideau; thoroughly renovated and is unsurpassed in all its appointments."

Figure 36: Street scene Merrickville, Ont. c. 1830. Note the substantial tavern on the left side of the sketch.

Figure 37: The former "Merrick Tavern" dates back to 1830 when it was constructed on the north bank of the Rideau Canal, where it still stands.

Figure 38: The "City Hotel", hosted by James Armstrong 1855 to 1885. Site of the first Council meeting of Village of Merrickville, Ont. In 1860.

CONCLUSION

The loss of the British possessions in America during the Revolutionary War ending in 1783 and the nearly similar experience by Britain in the War of 1812 with the United States, profoundly impacted Britain. Strategic military thinking became central in its approach to Canada. Communities along the border were vulnerable to attack and seizure by the Americans. The loyalty of the inhabitants of Upper Canada to Britain was suspect – most of them were from the United States and many held democratic ideals.

A second tier of defense and settlement was necessary, complete with a strong transportation linkage to provide safe internal movement of goods and people. Connecting Kingston on Lake Ontario with the Ottawa River on the other end, by using the existing water corridors of the Cataraqui and Rideau River systems, made sense. Construction of the Rideau Canal with fortifications and military settlements along the route was the answer. Implementation of this strategy began in 1823 with preliminary surveys and accelerated with the arrival of Colonel By in Hull in 1826.

Former military men were offered land and assistance to settle along the Rideau River corridor. Town sites were surveyed along the water corridor at Bytown (Ottawa), Richmond, Franktown and Perth and land grants given to military pensioners.

Notwithstanding the fact that ex-military personnel undoubtedly would be loyal, trustworthy settlers in Upper Canada, they were not entirely suited to the hardships of clearing isolated bush farms. Military life and training had provided them with a dependent life style. For instance, their daily ration of beer money had made many of them dependent on alcohol. Cultural attitudes of the Scottish, English and Irish settlers looked on alcohol as a necessity in their daily lives and did not frown upon excessive consumption as being necessarily wrong.

Many of these settlers were middle aged or older. They often did not have the youth, vigor or frontier skills that previous American settlers brought with them. Hiring labourers to clear their farms proved difficult because of the expense and difficulty in finding help.

As a result, they retreated to nearby taverns where they could commiserate with their comrades and find companionship from their isolated and harsh circumstances. Their pensions and daily "beer money" would sustain them. Alcoholism became almost an epidemic amongst former military personnel with premature death often being the outcome.

The economic development of the Rideau and Ottawa River corridors, combined with the poverty, misery and sectarian violence in Ireland, brought thousands of Irish emigrants to the Ottawa Valley. Employment on construction projects at the Lachine and Rideau Canals and in the burgeoning timber trade on the rivers attracted many Irish. Drinking was a way of life, together with recreational violence. Taverns were the social centres for them.

Finding themselves at the lowest social and economic level in early Upper Canadian society, some banded together in groups such as the "Shiners" to violently assert themselves for equality and recognition.

The Shiners "reign of terror" in the Bathurst District during the 1830's and early 1840's is unparalleled in Canadian history. Alcohol certainly provided the fuel to sustain it for over a decade.

Only changing attitudes and improved economic circumstances would break the hold that liquor had on early Canadian society.

ABOUT THE AUTHOR

Larry Cotton is a professional land use planner and historian, who lives in Lanark County. A passion for history and old stone houses provide the muse for his writing. Living in an area that has been settled much longer than many other parts of Ontario, provides a wealth of historical records to reference.

Over the years, Mr. Cotton has worked as a planner for the Counties of Renfrew and Stormont, Dundas and Glengarry. He also worked as a planner in the Barrie/Orillia area for a couple of municipalities. During his career he served as a Councillor for the Village of Winchester and the Township of Oro-Medonte and taught Municipal Administration at Georgian College.

Mr. Cotton has worked as a planning consultant for several municipalities in Eastern Ontario such as the former Township of Pakenham, Township of South Elmsley and the Township of Edwardsburg. This experience created a stronger understanding of the nature of some municipalities in Lanark, Leeds and Grenville Counties and the importance of further exploring their history.

INDEX

Griffith, Thomas

~H~
Hall, Adam
Hast, James
Harbison, David
Hast, James
Hennessy, Martin
Hill, Andrew
Hill, Maria
Hobbs, Mr. & Mrs.
Hog's Back
Hollahan, John
Hollenback, Nathan
Hollister, Charles
Holmes, Andrew
Holahan, Michael
Hughton, John
Humphries, Wm.

~J~
Jackson, James
Jamieson, R.S.
Johnston, Fanny
Johnston, James
Johnston, Noble
Johnston, Thomas
Joynt, John L.

~K~
Kars Village
Keenan, Const. Michael
Kelly, Wm.
Kemptville
Kemptville Brewery
Kerr, Robert
Kidd, Wm.
Kimberley Hotel
Kirk, Joseph

~L~
Leach, J.W.
LeBreton, Capt. John
Lefevre, James B.
Lett, Wm. P.

Lewis, Capt. John
Little, John
Loney, Elizabeth
Loney, Robert
Long Island
Lucas, G.
Lyon, Capt. George
Lyon, Robert
Lyon, Robinson
Lyon, Thomas

~M~
Macaulay, Thomas
MacNab, D. R.
Magee, Charles
Magee, Wm.
Malcolmson, Robert
Malone, Pat,
Manotick
Manotick Hotel
Marlborough House
Masonic Arms
McArthur, Peter
McCarnen, Bernard
McCaffrey, John
McCurdy, Joseph
McCullough, Daniel
McDonald, Angus
McDonnell, James
McEwen, Alexander
McEvoy, Samuel
McFarlane, Donald
McGee, Archibald
McGinty, "Mother"
McGregor, Wm.
McIntyre, Bridget
McIntyre, Daniel
McKay, Thomas
McLees, James
McMartin, Daniel
McNaughton, Michael
McPherson, George
McTaggart, John
McWhitcomb, R.
Merrickville

Moodie, Robert
Moore, Frederick A.
Moore, Wm.
Murdoch, Wm.
Murray, James
Murray, Thomas

~N~
Nepean
North Gower
North Gower Exchange Hotel
Nowlan, Patrick

~O~
O'Brien, James
OBrien, Patrick
O'Connor, Daniel
O'Grady, Michael
O'Neil, Daniel
Olmstead, Richard
Olmstead, Rufus

~P~
Paget, Thomas
Palace Hotel
Percival, Walter
Perkins, Henry
Pierce, John
Powell, Robert

~Q~
Quinlan, Patrick
Quinlan, Thomas

~R~
Reid, Wm.
Reilly, Edward
Reilly, Hugh
Reilly, John
Rickey, Hezekiah
Richmond
Richmond Landing
Richmond Road

~ Index ~

Rideau Hall
Rideau House
Robertson, John
Ross, George
Russell House
Ryan, Edward
Ryan, Jeremiah
Ryan, Jerry

~S~
Sellick, James

Sellick, John
"Shiners"
Smith, Ralph
Sparks, Nicholas
Steel, John
Stewart, John

~U~
Union House
Union Hotel

~W~
Ward, James
Warren, Thomas
Wellington Hotel
Wickham, Thomas
White, Charlie
Wight, James
Wood, Edmund
Wood, Wm. D.
Young, James

ENDNOTES

[1] Haydon, Andrew "Pioneer Sketches in the District of Bathurst" p.66

[2] Bathurst Courier, September 1, 1828

[3] W.A. Austin, C.E. Provincial Land Surveyor. W.C. Chewitt & Co. Ruggles Wright Esq. Library and Archives Canada. NMC 20966

[4] *Bathurst Courier, March 11, 1859*

[5] Leggett, Robert "Rideau Waterway" p. 204

[6] Leggett, Robert "Rideau Waterway" p. 204

[7] Ibid. p.79

[8] Ibid. p. 76

[9] Brockville Recorder, May 11, 1830

[10] Ibid. p. 76

[11] Brockville, Recorder, May 11, 1830

[12] Perth Examiner, February 12, 1830

[13] Brockville Recorder, November 8, 1833

[14] Toronto Globe, December 25, 1856

[15] Cross, Michael S. "The Shiner's War: Social Violence in the Ottawa Valley in the 1830's.

[16] Bathurst Courier, May 15, 1835

[17] Bathurst Courier, May 29, 1835

[18] Bathurst Courier, June 5, 1835

[19] Bathurst Courier, June 5, 1835

[20] Public Archives of Canada, Upper Canada Sundries, vol. 152, G.W. Baker to Rowan, June 15, 1835.

[21] Public Archives of Canada Upper Canada Sundries, vol. 156, Petition of the Grand Jury of Bathurst District to Sir John Colborne, August 1835

[22] Bytown Gazette, August 11, 1836

[23] Bathurst Courier, October 18, 1837

[24] Bathurst Courier, April 25, 1838

[25] Bathurst Courier, July 10, 1835

[26] Toronto Globe, December 25, 1856

[27] Bytown Gazette, October 20, 1836

[28] Bathurst Courier, July 10, 1835

[29] Bathurst Courier, February 23, 1837

[30] Bathurst Courier, September 29, 1837

[31] Bathurst Courier, July 21, 1846

[32] Bathurst Courier, October 2, 1835

[33] Bathurst Courier, September 29, 1837

[34] Ibid. p.11.

[35] Public Archives of Canada. "Upper Canada Sundries", vol. 159, George Baker to Rowan, November 17, 1835

[36] Bathurst Courier, December 11, 1835

[37] Bytown Gazette, August 18, 1836

[38] Guillet, Edwin C. "Early Pioneer Inns and Taverns Vol. 2" p. 144

[39] Brockville Recorder, November 8, 1833

[40] Bytown Gazette, August 6, 1840

[41] Guillet, Edwin C. Vol. 2, p. 149

[42] Bytown Gazette, June 19, 1839

[43] Montreal Canadian Courant, September 8, 1830

[44] Bytown Gazette, September 17, 1840

[45] Bytown Gazette, January 5, 1837

[46] Bytown Gazette, November 11, 1841

[47] Bathurst Courier, January 15, 1841

[48] Carleton Place Herald, June 25, 1862

[49] Almonte Express, August 2, 1861

[50] Op Cit, p. 69

[51] Bathurst Courier, July 1, 1836

[52] Perth Courier, February 25, 1853

[53] Walker, Harry and Olive "Carlton Saga" Runge Press Limited, Ottawa, 1968 p. 497

[54] Guillet, Edwin "Pioneer Inns and Taverns" Vol. 2 pps.122-125

[55] Ibid. p. 128.

[56] Lindsay, Coral "Kars on the Rideau Canal" Tweedsmuir History Committee, Kars Branch of the Women's Institute. 1972

[57] Rideau Township Branch Ottawa Archives "Tweedsmuir History of Kars" Volume Nine, North Gower, Ontario, 1972.

[58] Walker, Harry and Olive "Carleton Saga" p. 353

[59] McKenzie, Ruth "Leeds and Grenville" McClelland and Stewart Limited, Toronto/Montreal, 1967 p. 87

[60] Brockville Recorder, January 12, 1830

[61] Carleton Place Herald, December 24, 1873

[62] Carleton Place Herald, June 17, 1874

[63] Welch, Edwin ed. "Yankees and Loyalists: Bytown to Kingston in 1830". Bytown Museum, Ottawa. 1979. pp. 7-8

ENDNOTES

[64] Humphreys, Barbara A. "The Architectural Heritage of the Rideau Corridor"p. 65

[65] Carleton Place Herald, November 12, 1862

[66] Ibid. p.12

[67] Brockville Recorder, November 10, 1831.

[68] Carleton Place Herald, August 31, 1864

[69] Almonte Express, August 9, 1861